Creating Infographics with Adobe Illustrator: Volume 3

Interactive Infographics and the Creative Cloud

Jennifer Harder

Apress®

Creating Infographics with Adobe Illustrator: Volume 3: Interactive Infographics and the Creative Cloud

Jennifer Harder
Delta, BC, Canada

ISBN-13 (pbk): 979-8-8688-0037-5
https://doi.org/10.1007/979-8-8688-0038-2

ISBN-13 (electronic): 979-8-8688-0038-2

Managing Director, Apress Media LLC: Welmoed Spahr
Acquisitions Editor: Spandana Chatterjee
Development Editor: James Markham
Editorial Assistant: Jessica Vakili

Cover designed by eStudioCalamar

Cover image designed by Freepik (www.freepik.com)

Distributed to the book trade worldwide by Springer Science+Business Media New York, 1 New York Plaza, Suite 4600, New York, NY 10004-1562, USA. Phone 1-800-SPRINGER, fax (201) 348-4505, e-mail orders-ny@ springer-sbm.com, or visit www.springeronline.com. Apress Media, LLC is a California LLC and the sole member (owner) is Springer Science + Business Media Finance Inc (SSBM Finance Inc). SSBM Finance Inc is a **Delaware** corporation.

For information on translations, please e-mail booktranslations@springernature.com; for reprint, paperback, or audio rights, please e-mail bookpermissions@springernature.com.

Apress titles may be purchased in bulk for academic, corporate, or promotional use. eBook versions and licenses are also available for most titles. For more information, reference our Print and eBook Bulk Sales web page at http://www.apress.com/bulk-sales.

Any source code or other supplementary material referenced by the author in this book is available to readers on GitHub. For more detailed information, please visit https://www.apress.com/gp/services/source-code.

Paper in this product is recyclable

Table of Contents

About the Author

Jennifer Harder has worked in the graphic design industry for over 15 years. She has a degree in graphic communications and is currently teaching Acrobat and Adobe Creative Cloud courses at Langara College. She is also the author of several Apress books and related videos.

About the Technical Reviewer

 **Sourabh Mishra** is an entrepreneur, developer, speaker, author, corporate trainer, and animator. He is a Microsoft guy; he is very passionate about Microsoft technologies and a true .NET warrior. Sourabh started his career when he was just 15 years old. He's loved computers since childhood. His programming experience includes C/C++, ASP.NET, C#, VB.NET, WCF, SQL Server, Entity Framework, MVC, Web API, Azure, jQuery, Highcharts, and Angular. He is also an expert in computer graphics. Sourabh is the author of the book *Practical Highcharts with Angular* published by Apress. Sourabh has been awarded a Most Valuable Professional (MVP) status. He has the zeal to learn new technologies, sharing his knowledge on several online community forums.

He is a founder of "IECE Digital" and "Sourabh Mishra Notes," an online knowledge-sharing platform where one can learn new technologies very easily and comfortably.

Acknowledgments

For their patience and advice, I would like to thank the following people, for without them I could never have written this book:

- My parents, for encouraging me to read large computer textbooks that would one day inspire me to write my own books.

- My dad, for reviewing the first draft before I sent a proposal.

- My program coordinator, Raymond Chow, at Langara College, who gave me the chance to teach evening courses and allowed me to find new and creative ways to teach software.

- My various freelance clients whose projects, while working on them, helped me research and learn more about various topics.

At Apress, I would like to thank Spandana Chatterjee and Mark Powers for showing me how to lay out a professional textbook and pointing out that even when you think you've written it all, there's still more to write. Also, thanks to the technical reviewer for providing encouraging comments. And thanks to the rest of the Apress team for being involved in the printing of this book and making my dream a reality again. I am truly grateful and blessed.

Introduction

Welcome to the book *Creating Infographics with Adobe Illustrator: Volume 3*. This book is the third of a three-volume set.

What This Book Is About

In Volume 1 of this book, the focus was on infographic basics, and in Volume 2, we explored working with graphs/charts as well as 3D effects using Illustrator's tools.

In this book, we will be looking at how to add interactivity to your Illustrator files as well as some thoughts on how to work with your clients on additional infographic ideas based on what you learned in Volumes 1 and 2. This book will also conclude by considering what other applications you should learn more about from the Creative Cloud so that you can continue to enhance and add more interactivity to your next project.

This book is divided into three chapters in which we will explore the steps of infographic creation regarding interactivity. Much of what you learn in this book can also be applied to logo creation. However, as you will have discovered in the past volumes, infographic creation often requires more invested research and time due to many factors that I will try to break down in this book. If you are a beginner to the idea of infographics, make sure to use Volume 1 to first focus on logo design or create a simple 2D infographic before moving on to more complex ideas like 3D and general page layout with text which was explored in Volume 2 and now Scalable Vector Graphics (SVG) in this volume. As you work along in this book on projects, if you are a student, make sure to consult with your instructor about their thoughts on infographics as well as work with your fellow classmates to discover what makes an ideal infographic. They may have different thoughts on this topic than myself that will be insightful as well.

Here is a brief overview of the chapters in this volume:

- **Chapter 1**: If you are designing an infographic for your website, then you may want to add some ability to scale the graphics and also add some hover interactivity when a viewer moves the mouse over a specific area to gain more information. Illustrator has these settings available with the application, using Scalable Vector Graphics (SVG) and the SVG Interactivity panel, and options for exporting the file. We will also be looking at how to place an SVG file on an HTML5 page using the application Adobe Dreamweaver.

- **Chapter 2**: This chapter focuses on what are the final steps for completing your infographics with your clients and also some additional ideas that you may want to explore and adapt for your next project. The designs are based on what was explored in the previous chapter and earlier volumes on the topics of 2D and 3D design.

- **Chapter 3**: This chapter looks at how you can save your Illustrator files for print. Then I will show you how to save them for the Web as assets, using the Export Assets panel. Next, we look at the Creative Cloud library using the Libraries panel to share your assets and graphics with other Adobe applications as well as others working on your project. I also show some examples of how you can further embellish your infographics in Photoshop, the setup of a basic layout for InDesign, and then discuss some other applications that you could use to make your infographics more interactive, such as Adobe Animate, as well as other video, 3D, and graphing-related Adobe applications and resources.

The data in this book that we will be using for the infographic design is purely fictitious and is subject to change. It is not meant to reflect any actual data, only act as a placeholder to display the graphic. For your own projects, you will want to have accurate and up-to-date data if you are going to present your infographic to the public.

Adobe Illustrator

Adobe Illustrator is one of the many drawing applications that is part of the collection of the Adobe Creative Cloud when you have a subscription with the company. Refer to Figure 1.

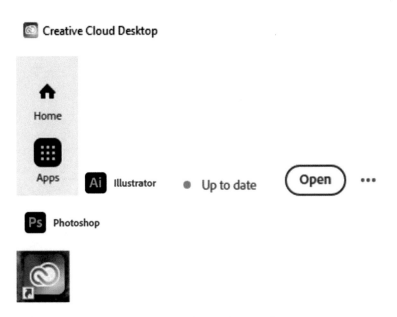

Figure 1. *Creative Cloud Desktop console and icon shortcut*

Note   In this volume, it is assumed you have already downloaded and installed the Creative Cloud Desktop as well as the applications of Photoshop and Illustrator. For more details on how to do this, refer back to Volume 1 and these next sections to review those steps.

The topics in this book do not cover Adobe Illustrator for the iPad.

While some people like working with a single software like Photoshop, I prefer Creative Cloud because it offers you access to many applications including the web application as well as other applications in my plan which included Adobe Color that we saw in Volume 1. Refer to Figure 2.

Figure 2. *Link to Adobe Color online application via the Creative Cloud*

If you have purchased and downloaded the Creative Cloud Desktop console from Adobe, you will want to install Illustrator along with Photoshop and InDesign on your desktop computer. You can refer to the section "System Requirements" if you need to first check if your device can handle these applications. Refer to Figure 3.

Figure 3. *Desktop application icons for Photoshop, Illustrator, and InDesign that you can install*

System Requirements

If you are unsure whether your computer meets the following requirements for running the latest version of Adobe Illustrator (version 27.9) on your Windows or macOS desktop computers, then please consult the following links:

https://helpx.adobe.com/download-install/kb/operating-system-guidelines.html

https://helpx.adobe.com/creative-cloud/system-requirements.html

https://helpx.adobe.com/illustrator/system-requirements.html

With the Creative Cloud Desktop console visible, the installation steps are similar for all Adobe applications on your computer. I will, in the next section, "Install and Open Application Steps," give a brief overview of how to load and open your Illustrator application.

In this volume, you should have by now installed Photoshop and Illustrator. We will be using Illustrator mostly throughout this book, but Photoshop will be mentioned in Chapter 3.

If you have downloaded Photoshop, this will have caused Camera Raw and possibly Bridge to download as well. That's OK. Though not required for this book, Camera Raw is a useful tool for color correction of photos. Bridge, as will be mentioned in Chapter 3, is great for keeping your images and photos organized and working with the Libraries panel. InDesign, which will further be discussed in Chapter 3, is a great layout application that can be used for incorporating graphics to create your final publication. Refer to Figures 3 and 4.

Figure 4. *Adobe application icons Camera Raw and Bridge*

At this point, if you have not used any other applications before, such as Animate, which comes with Media Encoder or Dreamweaver, download these as well to open and work with the projects in this book. For Dreamweaver, we will be using this application to add SVG files to an HTML5 web page. In Chapter 3, however, I will merely be mentioning how the Animate and Media Encoder applications could be used later to incorporate your original infographics to add more interactivity. Refer to Figure 5.

Figure 5. *Adobe application icons Animate, Media Encoder, and Dreamweaver*

Note Though optional for this book, for myself and my personal workflow, I also install Acrobat Pro, as this application can assist you in your graphics workflow for PDF file creation after completing your work in InDesign. We will look at this regarding creating file formats from Illustrator and InDesign files in Chapter 3. In addition, if you are doing a lot of video work, then you may also want to later install Premiere Pro, After Effects, and Audition for video and audio work. Though none of these are required for the book, they will be mentioned again in Chapter 3. Refer to Figure 6.

Figure 6. *Adobe application icons Acrobat Pro, Premiere Pro, After Effects, and Audition*

Install and Open Application Steps

If you have not already installed Photoshop or Illustrator on your computer, as mentioned in Volume 1, then do so now from the Creative Cloud console. Refer to Apps ➤ All Apps ➤ Desktop Tabs. Click the Install button beside each application one at a time. Refer to Figure 7.

Figure 7. *Use the Adobe Creative Apps Desktop area to install Photoshop and Illustrator*

The installation may take several minutes. You will then receive a notification once the installation is complete, and then from time to time, the Creative Cloud will send automatic updates to you as well as bug fixes. Some installations may require a computer restart. In the installed area, Photoshop and Illustrator will appear up to date. Then, to open, for example, Illustrator, just click the Open button on the same line. Refer to Figure 8.

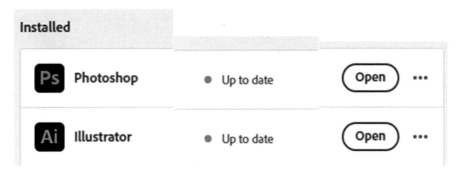

Figure 8. *Open these installed applications using the button*

The Illustrator application will then open after a minute, and then you will be presented with a desktop interface. We will look at this area more throughout the book. But for now, if you want to close the application, then choose from the preceding menu File ➤ Exit or Ctrl/CMD+Q, and Illustrator will close. Refer to Figure 9.

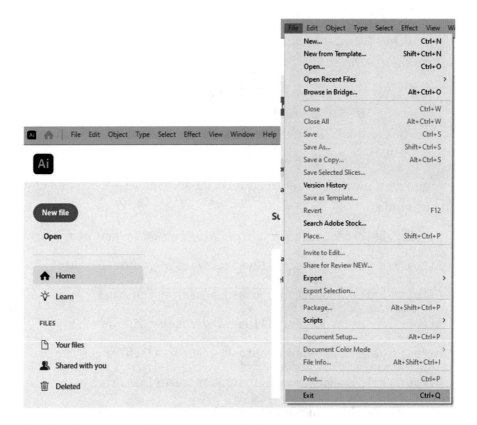

Figure 9. *Use Illustrator's File menu to exit Illustrator*

These are the same steps you can use with the Photoshop application, and then to close, use File ➤ Exit.

Additional Resources

While not required for this book, if you are interested in other related topics that I have written on Adobe applications, after you have read the three volumes on the topic of infographics, you might also want to view one of the following:

- *Graphics and Multimedia for the Web with Adobe Creative Cloud: Navigating the Adobe Software Landscape*

- *Accurate Layer Selections Using Photoshop's Selection Tools: Use Photoshop and Illustrator to Refine Your Artwork*

- *Perspective Warps and Distorts with Adobe Tools: Volume 1: Putting a New Twist on Photoshop*

- *Perspective Warps and Distorts with Adobe Tools: Volume 2: Putting a New Twist on Illustrator*

- *Data Merge and Styles for Adobe InDesign CC 2018: Creating Custom Documents for Mailouts and Presentation Packages*: While this is an older book, you could certainly use it to incorporate some of your graphic designs in future layout projects that involve mass mail-outs.

Also, for the most up-to-date information, make sure to use Adobe online help links which can be found at

- https://helpx.adobe.com/photoshop/using/whats-new.html
- https://helpx.adobe.com/illustrator/using/whats-new.html
- https://helpx.adobe.com/photoshop/user-guide.html
- https://helpx.adobe.com/illustrator/user-guide.html
- https://helpx.adobe.com/photoshop/tutorials.html
- https://helpx.adobe.com/illustrator/tutorials.html

I will be referring to these links throughout the book if you need additional information on a specific tool or panel. However, the focus of the book will be mostly on Illustrator, and it is assumed that you have some experience already with Photoshop.

You can also find these links in the Creative Cloud Desktop console when you hover over them in the installed area and click the icon. Refer to Figure 10.

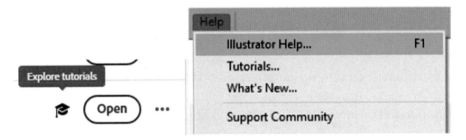

Figure 10. *Adobe Creative Cloud and Help menu links to additional resources*

Or you can access similar areas in the Illustrator Help drop-down menu or the Discover panel that can be accessed via a magnifying glass icon when a file is open. The same settings are available in Photoshop as well, which are helpful for speeding up your workflow. Refer to Figure 11.

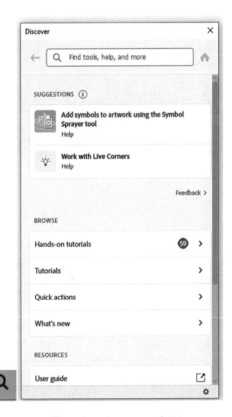

Figure 11. *Adobe Illustrator application icon and Discover panel*

For the InDesign application, you can find a similar panel under Window ➤ Learn or refer to the Lightbulb icon. Refer to Figure 12.

Figure 12. *Adobe InDesign application icon and Learn panel*

For tutorials in Dreamweaver, Animate, and Media Encoder, refer to the Help menu for that specific application.

Now that you are a bit more familiar with how to install and open Photoshop and Illustrator and have worked with Volumes 1 and 2, let's continue our journey into infographic creation.

For this book, you can find the following project files for each chapter at this link: `http://github.com/apress/illustrator-basics`

CHAPTER 1

Interactive Infographics with SVG

In this chapter, you will learn how to create basic interactivity for your infographic online using SVG (Scalable Vector Graphics) files.

Illustrator, unlike Photoshop, does not have the option to create any form of animation like GIF or video file, to create an animated infographic for the Web. However, you can create some basic interactivity using an SVG file which will allow you to hover over areas of a graphic to reveal a color change or text information. While working with Illustrator, you do not have to be a coding expert or know a lot about SVG files to get started. This chapter will explore some SVG Interactivity possibilities and the process of creating an SVG file. Later, we will also explore how this can be applied to a few similar projects.

Note   This chapter does contain projects that can be found in the Volume 3 Chapter 1 folder. Some of the text in this chapter in regard to SVG has been adapted and updated from my earlier book *Graphics and Multimedia for the Web with Adobe Creative Cloud*.

What Is SVG?

There are two kinds of file formats: SVG (.svg) and SVG compressed (.svgz).

Scalable Vector Graphics are based on XML coding vector image format for two-dimensional graphics with support for interactivity and animation. They can also be used to create colorful types for the Web, which can also be displayed on handheld

© Jennifer Harder 2023
J. Harder, *Creating Infographics with Adobe Illustrator: Volume 3*,
https://doi.org/10.1007/979-8-8688-0038-2_1

devices. These vector images can be scaled to any size and keep their basic form without losing quality, while other raster formats like JPG, GIF, or PNG files would appear pixelated if scaled up and their file size is often compressed, and information is discarded, becoming also known as "lossy." However, SVGs are generally considered "lossless" or don't compress much, and no major information is discarded to cause image degradation. The exception is compressed SVG (.svgz) that can be 20%–50% of the original size.

In this chapter, our focus is on SVG files which are ideal for logos and infographics with simple colorful designs that are not overly detailed.

To create an SVG file, you need to start with a graphic design that you created and saved in Illustrator as an (.ai) or (.eps) file. In this case, we are focused on using the (.ai) file.

To prepare to create an SVG file, some additional considerations and care must be taken upon completion of the final design. For example, you need to decide exactly what kind of basic interactivity is available, how to set up that interactivity using the SVG Interactivity panel, and how that relates to the organization of your layers and sublayers, which we will explore in a basic version next.

Note   Examples of SVG color fonts used by Adobe are Trajan Color, Noto Color Emoji SVG, and EmojiOne Color. Refer to this page for more details.

`https://helpx.adobe.com/fonts/using/ot-svg-color-fonts.html`

SVG Interactivity Panel

When you create SVG files for the Web, they are scalable or responsive, so they will not become pixelated like GIF, JPEG, or PNG images. These bitmap or raster file types can be used to create graphic buttons or rollovers on a website and can be programmed in an application like Dreamweaver on an HTML5 web page. However, you can also create an SVG image that can act like a button when saved or exported for a web page. You can find the panel under Window ➤ SVG Interactivity. Refer to Figure 1-1.

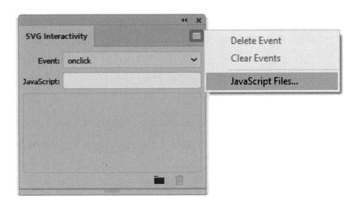

Figure 1-1. *The SVG Interactivity panel*

We will look at the details of this panel in a moment. However, as mentioned, to use the SVG Interactivity panel correctly, you must first design your images in an AI or EPS file. In this example, under File ➤ Open locate and open the file tool_identification.ai, and use it as a reference. Notice that before I began, I made sure to give each of my layers and sublayers a distinct name as the JavaScript code used in the panel will regard these layers or sublayers as an object with an ID. Refer to Figure 1-2.

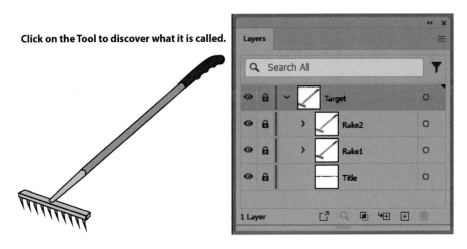

Figure 1-2. *Each layer that will interact must be named distinctly in the Layers panel*

The Target layer has technically three sublayers: the Title which is the lowest sublayer; Rake1 layer, which is a grouped image of the rake in color; and Rake2, which is a grouped image of the rake but in grayscale. My goal in this example is to have the ability for the whole rake to change color when the target area is hovered over and if clicked upon to see an alert message pop up.

Note that for this project, I also edited and scaled my artboard using the Artboard tool (described in Volume 1 Chapter 5) so that it was smaller and hence would not take up a lot of space on the website. To scale, I used the bounding box handles and the Control panel; I made it 3.75 inches in width and 3.75 inches in height. Though for the Web, you may prefer to work in pixels rather than inch settings. Remember to adjust your rulers by right-clicking them if you need to switch. Use View ➤ Rulers ➤ Show Rulers if not visible. Refer to Figure 1-3.

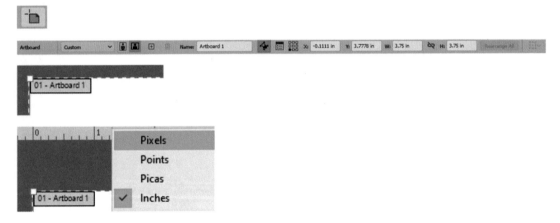

Figure 1-3. *Artboard tool active and Artboard settings in the Control panel*

Remember to click the Hand tool in the Toolbars panel to exit that area and return to normal editing mode. Refer to Figure 1-4.

Figure 1-4. *Use the Hand tool to exit Artboard mode*

Your artboard page size for SVG projects will vary depending on what you plan for your HTML page website and the space that you plan to display your artwork.

Also, in this case, I design the file in CMYK color mode. However, when I create my SVG file, it will convert to RGB color mode automatically. Because I am using website-compatible colors from the Swatches panel, the change should be very minimal. However, if you are unsure how the color will appear, it would be best to start with a new file (.ai) in RGB color mode.

If you are not designing the website page where the SVG file will be displayed, make sure to consult with the web designer for exact sizing and color questions. In this chapter, we will be focusing on the very basic HTML settings so that you will get an idea of how the SVG file functions in a browser.

For your own project, once you have completed your layout of the (.ai) file, the next step would be to choose one of the following options:

- File ➤ Save As.

- File ➤ Export ➤ Export As.

- Or use one of the other options described later in more detail in this chapter under sections "Option 1 and Option 2." Refer to Figure 1-5.

In this case, we will use the Save As option 1. Make sure to save the SVG file somewhere on your computer desktop. Click Save and make sure to give the file a name, and then continue to the next dialog box. Refer to Figure 1-5.

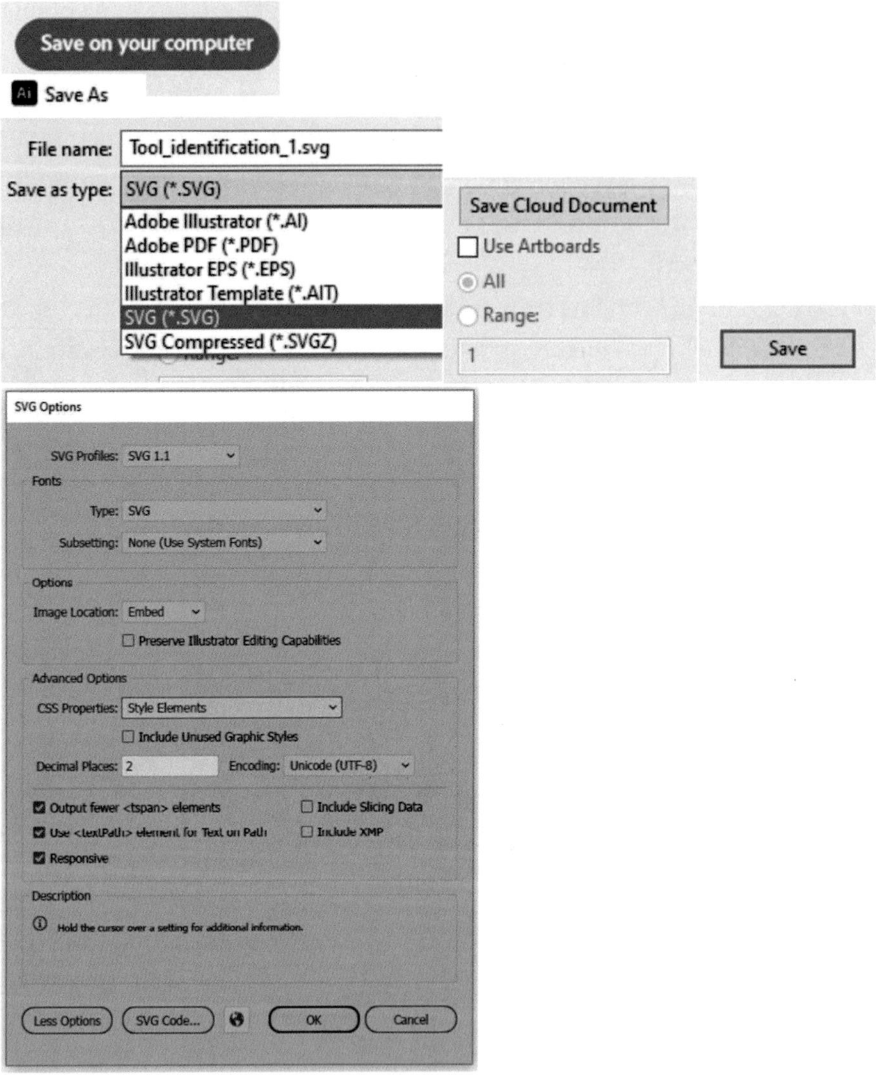

Figure 1-5. *Save your SVG file and SVG Options dialog box*

Note   Export As (see Option 2) gives similar settings, but they are more simplified, and you may prefer this dialog box as you can set the Object IDs to Layer Names. Click Export to continue to the next dialog box. Refer to Figure 1-6.

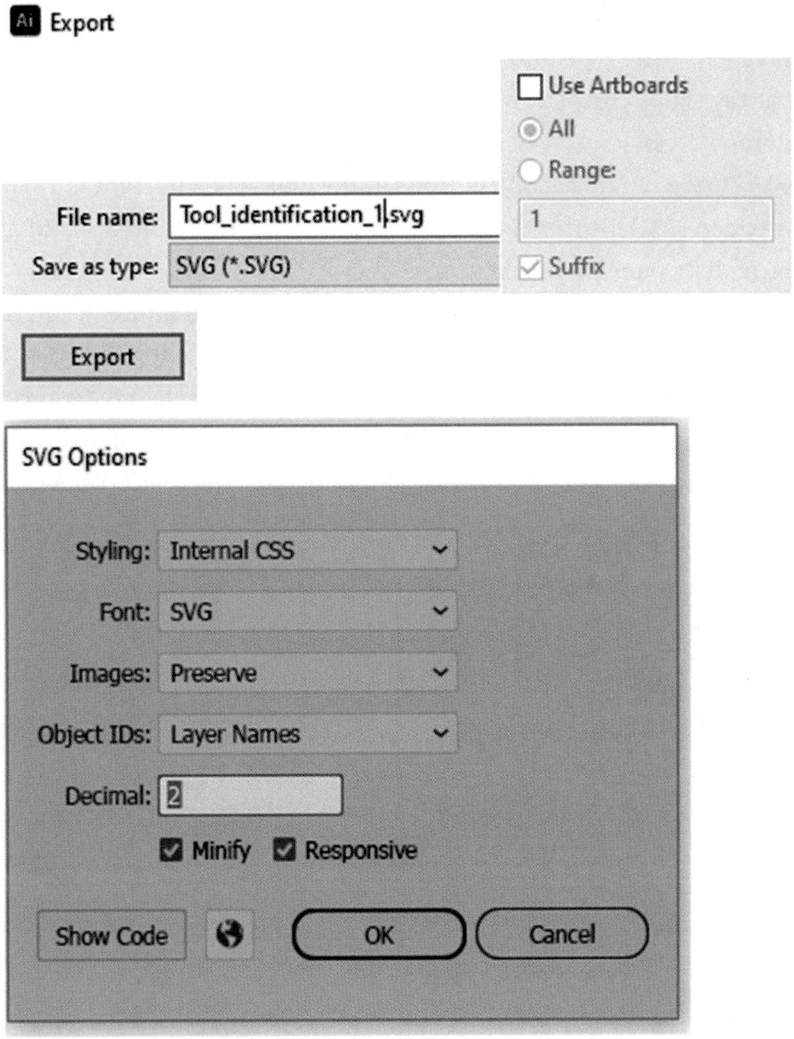

Ai Export

☐ Use Artboards
◉ All
◯ Range:

File name: | Tool_identification_1|svg | | 1 |

Save as type: | SVG (*.SVG) | ☑ Suffix

Export

SVG Options

Styling: | Internal CSS ⌄ |

Font: | SVG ⌄ |

Images: | Preserve ⌄ |

Object IDs: | Layer Names ⌄ |

Decimal: | 2 |

☑ Minify ☑ Responsive

Show Code | 🌐 | OK | Cancel

Figure 1-6. *Save your SVG settings*

We will look at these settings in more detail later. At this point, just make sure that your responsive setting is enabled.

Once done, click OK in the dialog box to Save your new SVG file in a folder. You can look at my finished file, Tool_identification._1.svg. Keep this file open for the moment.

As mentioned, in this example, we are going to first look at how to create a simple informational message when this item is hovered over to describe what it is.

Once the file is in the SVG format, only then can you work with the SVG Interactivity panel. Any JavaScript you type into this SVG Interactivity panel, while in the AI or EPS file, will not always copy correctly into the SVG, so it is very crucial to follow these steps if you want interactivity in your SVGs. You can check if code has been added during export if you go to SVG Code or Show Code buttons in the dialog box in Figures 1-5 or 1-6. You will see in the open (.txt) file that no actions were applied if you did not add any event to this SVG Interactivity panel in the original EPS or AI file.

If you do not have the file open already, open the newly created SVG file Tool_ identification._1.svg in Illustrator to enter one or more of the following event triggers and JavaScript into the panel. For this example, make sure to select the top Layer on the Target as I have in Figure 1-2, where I clicked on the circle and made it appear with a double ring. This will select all the layers, including the type in the Title. Refer to Figure 1-7.

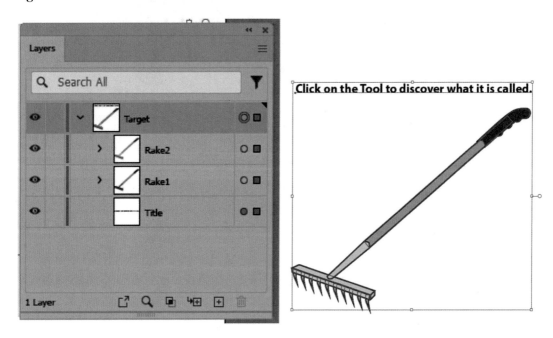

Figure 1-7. *The target must be selected in the Layers panel before you can enter any JavaScript in the SVG Interactivity panel*

With the target selected, you can now start entering information in the SVG Interactivity panel. Let's review the panel first.

The following command or event triggers are available for SVG elements. Refer to Figure 1-8.

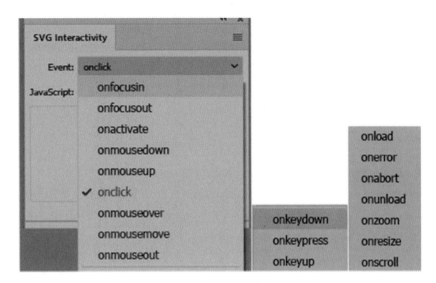

Figure 1-8. *Event triggers in the SVG Interactivity panel will only work when you are in an SVG file*

Elements

onfocusin: Trigger the JavaScript action when the element receives focus, such as selection by the pointer when you click on that element.

onfocusout: Trigger the JavaScript action when the SVG element loses focus, often when another element receives focus, or when you click off that element.

onactivate: Trigger the JavaScript action with a mouse click or keypress, depending upon the element.

onmousedown: Trigger the JavaScript action when the mouse button is pressed down over an element.

onmouseup: Trigger the JavaScript action when the mouse button is released over an element.

onclick: Trigger the JavaScript action when the mouse is clicked over an element.

onmouseover: Trigger the JavaScript action when the pointer is moved onto an element.

onmousemove: Trigger the JavaScript action while the pointer is over an element.

onmouseout: Trigger the JavaScript action when the pointer is moved away from an element.

onkeydown: Trigger the JavaScript action when a key is pressed down.

onkeypress: Trigger the JavaScript action while a key is pressed down.

onkeyup: Trigger the JavaScript action when a key is released.

Document

onload: Trigger the JavaScript action after the SVG document has been completely parsed by the browser. Use this type of event to call onetime-only initialization functions.

onerror: Trigger the JavaScript action when an element does not load properly or another error occurs.

onabort: Trigger the JavaScript action when the page loading is stopped before the element is completely loaded.

onunload: Trigger the JavaScript action when the SVG document is removed from a window or frame.

onzoom: Trigger the JavaScript action when the zoom level is changed for the document.

onresize: Trigger the JavaScript action when the document view is resized.

onscroll: Trigger the JavaScript action when the document view is scrolled or panned.

When the mouse or button is released, whatever action you applied will occur.

Each event must be entered one at a time into the SVG Interactivity panel, along with the JavaScript, and then click in the lower box to confirm it. Refer to Figure 1-9.

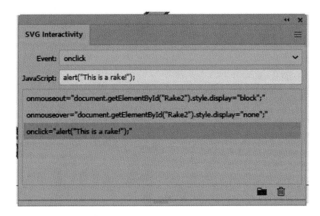

Figure 1-9. *Event triggers in the SVG Interactivity panel will only work when you are in an SVG file*

Here are some scripts that I added to my graphic in order to cause the appearance of a slight color change when the sublayer shows/hides and a message to appear when clicking the part of the image:

```
onmouseout="document.getElementById("Rake2").style.display="block";"
```

```
onmouseover="document.getElementById("Rake2").style.display="none";"
```

```
onclick="alert("This is a rake!");"
```

The only part that you must write is the JavaScript without the outer straight quotes, and Illustrator does the rest. For example:

You would select the Event onclick from the drop-down menu and then type into the JavaScript text box:

```
alert("This is a rake!");
```

Then click into the lower code area to confirm.

You would repeat these steps one at a time for

- **onmouseout**: You would type

  ```
  document.getElementById("Rake2").style.display="block";
  ```

- **onmouseover**: You would type

  ```
  document.getElementById("Rake2").style.display="none";
  ```

In this case, we use this code to show (block) and hide (none) the upper Rake2 image, which is using the document's Layer "Rake2" name as its ID Element that it is controlling. The alert is not set to any sublayer, but the event will occur when you click on the overall target as you will see shortly.

If at any point you need to make a change, select that code line in the SVG Interactivity panel and alter the text, then click another line in the code area to confirm the change. To delete a script, select it and click the panel's trash can icon. The SVG Interactivity panel will only allow you to enter one event per target, so you cannot enter an event twice. Refer to Figure 1-9.

On your own project, at this point, once you have completed your code, you would File ➤ Save your SVG in Illustrator. In this example, the code is already typed, so you can close the file without saving changes.

For the file and script mentioned, if you test the file in a browser, it will allow you to hide and show a color change of the rake as you move your mouse in and out of the browser area. Then, when you click on the rake, a message or alert is revealed. This testing is only possible in a browser and not in Illustrator, so for your own projects, you may have to open your own SVG file a few times in Illustrator and save the file if you need to adjust the script again before refreshing and testing again in the browser. Refer to Figure 1-10.

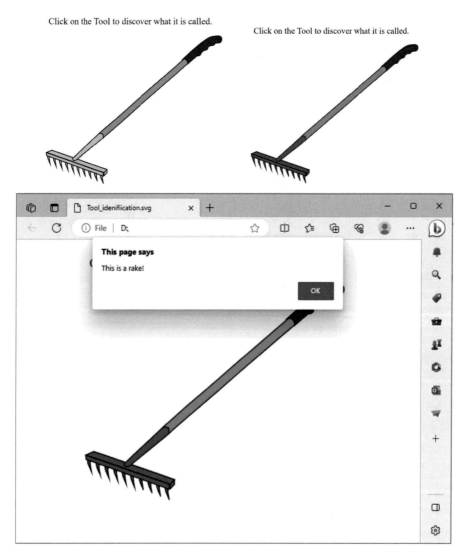

Figure 1-10. *The mouse can now interact with the SVG file in the browser*

Notice that if you scale your SVG in the browser, it never loses its shape. It will shrink and grow in size as you adjust your browser if you set your Options to responsive. Later, using Dreamweaver, I will just show you how to modify your HTML code so that you can create an example of a slightly scaled SVG so that it does not take up the whole page, as it will when you open the SVG directly in the browser.

Adding Additional Linked Scripts

To add additional JavaScript to the SVG Interactivity panel that is linked to the events, click the folder in the lower right of the panel or choose JavaScript Files from the SVG Interactivity panel's menu. This opens the JavaScript Files dialog box.

This will open the JavaScript Files dialog box as in Figure 1-11.

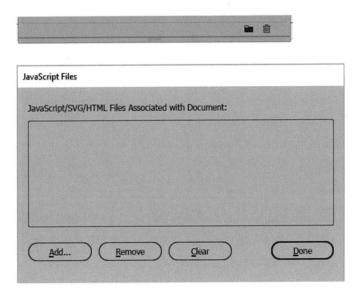

Figure 1-11. *The JavaScript Files dialog box*

Clicking the Add button will allow you to access the dialog box to add a URL link to some external JavaScript (.js) that you might use for additional interaction that relates to the event in your file on your website. Refer to Figure 1-12.

Figure 1-12. *Add JavaScript File dialog box, and click choose link to an external JavaScript File*

Clicking choose will allow you to search for and add a link to the associated JavaScript file (.js) that contains the JavaScript Actions and add that information to the file.

If you have a file to add for your project, click OK to complete the link. For this project, click Cancel as we are not focused on advanced JavaScript for this book.

For your own project, if you later want to unlink that file, press the Remove or Clear buttons (Figure 1-11). Leave this area blank for now. Then click Done to exit.

For your own projects, make sure to File ➤ Save your SVG file. Later in the chapter, we will look at an example of how to add it to an HTML page.

Tip   If you are not sure what effects to use and you want scalable shading, use the SVG filters. They are found in the main menu under Effect ➤ SVG filters and are great for creating effects like blurs and shadows. Once you apply a filter to a selected object, you can change it, in the Appearance panel, by clicking it and choosing a different filter from the menu while you preview it. You can appy more than one filter at a time. Refer to Figure 1-13 as an example.

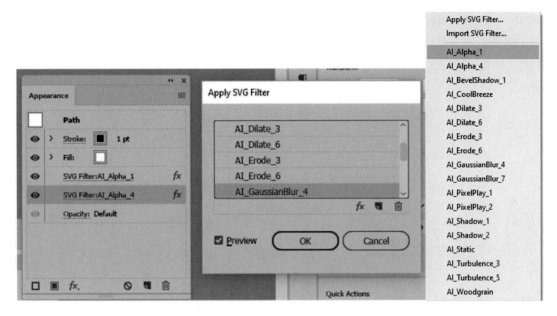

Figure 1-13. *The Appearance panel will allow you to alter your SVG filters quickly*

For infographics try, AI_BevelShadow _1, AI_Shadow_1, and AI_Shadow_2. They are good for drop shadow effects. For blur or feather try AI_GaussianBlur_4 and AI_GaussianBlur_7.

SVG filters can also be added (imported) and adapted if you have files from a client or coworker that have advanced coding skills in SVG using the Import SVG Filter menu selection. Refer to Figure 1-13.

Option 1: Creating and Saving an SVG Infographic (File ➤ Save As or File ➤ Save a Copy)

Now that you understand a bit more about the SVG creation workflow and you understand the steps of how the SVG Interactivity panel works, you can then use JavaScript to interact with your shapes on Target layers in simple or complex events. Let's, however, return to the settings for saving a copy of your Illustrator file as an SVG when you use the File ➤ Save As and select SVG as your Save As Type after selecting a location to save your file (do not check the Use Artboards check box) and click Save in the dialog box and review the SVG Options dialog box in more detail. Refer to Figure 1-5 and Figure 1-14.

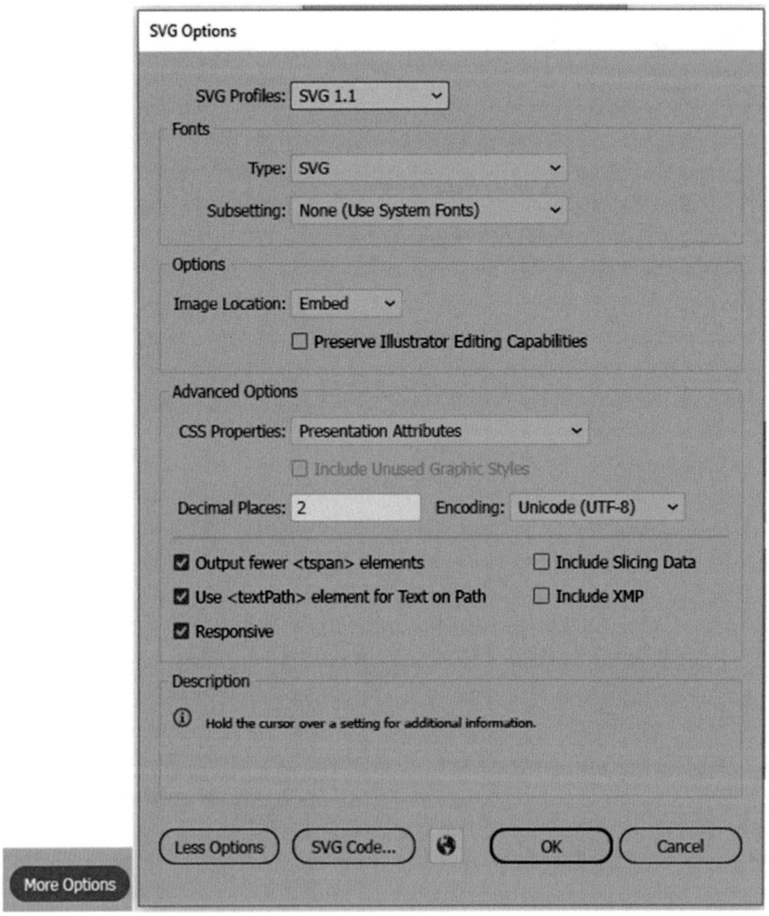

Figure 1-14. *SVG Options dialog box with Advanced Options*

You can also use the File ➤ Save a Copy options, and this will get you to the SVG Options dialog box as seen in Figure 1-14. Either way, click the More/Less Options button to expand the dialog box.

Note   If you want to work with more than one file format at a time, choose Export for Screens which you will look at Option 2 of this chapter.

Now let's look at the Options in more detail.

SVG Profiles: SVG has various precreated presets you can use, depending on your compression settings. Some settings are better for mobile phones. In this case, we are using the default setting of SVG 1.1 since we are just viewing it in the browser. You can learn more about each setting in the Description area as you hover over your selection. Refer to Figure 1-15.

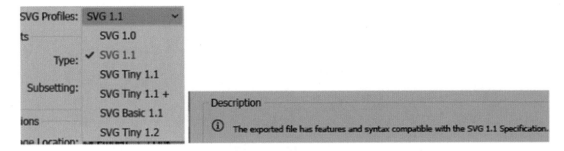

Figure 1-15. *SVG Options dialog box Profile settings*

Fonts: If your SVG file contains fonts, you can set them to either type: SVG or a graphic outline. Convert to outline will make the text non-editable later. Using outline will maintain the general look of your original font though it might alter during scaling. When you use the setting of SVG, you are relying on your computer's system fonts or whatever setting you set from the Subsetting List. Subsetting allows only some or all font characters or glyphs to be loaded into the file that could be All or various options of Common Roman and Common English Glyphs as in Figure 1-16. In this case, I am just using SVG and the Subsetting of None (Use System Fonts); this may cause my browser, for example, the Myriad Pro font, to change to something like Times Roman or a serif font.

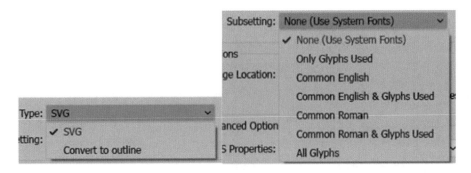

Figure 1-16. *SVG Options dialog box Font settings for Type and Subsetting*

If you choose Use System Fonts, the user's computer will interpret how the fonts appear when viewed on their screen. A setting like All Glyphs should retain the shape of the font you used in the file.

Options determines if images are embedded or linked to the file or to preserve. You can also set whether Illustrator can continue to edit the image file after it has been saved as an SVG. If no images are in the Illustrator file and just your vector graphics, you can just leave this at the default of Embed and leave Preserve Illustrator Editing Capabilities unchecked. Refer to Figure 1-17.

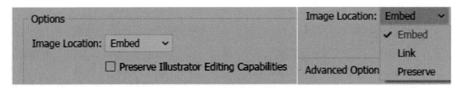

Figure 1-17. *SVG Options dialog box Option settings*

Advanced Options: When the More Options button is clicked, you will see these additional options. Refer to Figure 1-18.

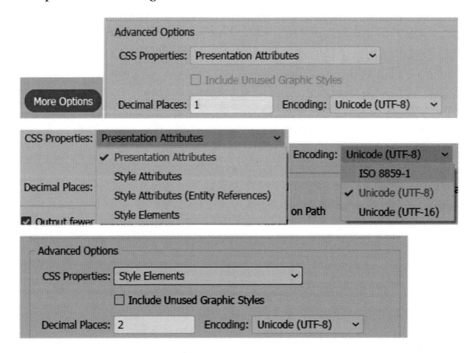

Figure 1-18. *SVG Options dialog box Advanced settings*

CSS Properties refers to how the CSS (cascading style sheets) will style themselves within the code. For a more detailed description of each, you can hover over each one and view the definition in the lower description area of the dialog box. CSS is often used with HTML and JavaScript to add color and other graphic enhancements styling. You can choose from the following options:

- **Presentation Attributes**: Applies properties at the highest point in the hierarchy, which allows for the most flexibility for specific edits and transformations.

- **Style Attributes**: Creates the most readable files but may increase file size. This code is used in transformations, such as the Extensible Stylesheet Language Transformation (XSLT).

- **Style Attributes (Entity References)**: Results in faster rendering times and reduced file sizes.

- **Style Elements**: Is the best option when creating a single style sheet that formats both HTML and SVG documents. This may result in slower rendering speeds.

In my case, I use the setting of Style Elements rather than Presentation Attributes.

If unused Graphic Styles are present in the design, you have the option to include them when using the CSS properties options of Style Attributes (Entity References) and Style Elements; otherwise, this option is not available. Refer to Figure 1-18.

Decimal Places: Refers to how precise the vector will be in the artwork. You can set it from 1 to 7, a high value results in a larger file. A setting of 2 or 3 is best. Refer to Figure 1-18.

Encoding: Refers to the type of coding used for the SVG file. The default is Unicode (UTF-8). However, you can set ISO 8859-1 and Unicode (UTF-16). Refer to Figure 1-18.

A few more options in this dialog box are presented here in Figure 1-19. Hovering over them will give you a description in the lower part of the dialog box.

☑ Output fewer <tspan> elements   ☐ Include Slicing Data

☑ Use <textPath> element for Text on Path   ☐ Include XMP

☑ Responsive

Description

ⓘ Outputs fewer <tspan> elements which will reduce file size. Appearance may change
    due to ignoring kerning position.

Figure 1-19. *SVG Options dialog box Advanced settings*

Selecting the following options:

Output fewer <tspan> elements: Will reduce the file size, but it may alter the text or overall image slightly such as ignoring kerning position in the text.

Use <textPath> element for Text on Path: If you want to preserve text on a path object, otherwise each character will be written as a <text> element. Checked this will keep the xml code more compact, but it may not accurately preserve the appearance shown in the Illustrator document.

Responsive: Allows the CSS to make the SVG image scalable in the browser, this is a good option for scalable websites.

Include Slicing Data: If the image includes slices, the location and optimization setting will be preserved.

Include XMP: This allows the SVG to include important metadata like "author" "date created" and "date modified." Some of this information is found in your original AI file when you go to File ➤ File Info and review that dialog box.

If you click Less Options, this hides the Advanced features. The SVG Code button reveals the code to review as text (.txt), and you could use a text editor like Notepad++ or Dreamweaver to edit your SVG Code further if you copied and pasted it into a (.html) file. Refer to Figure 1-20.

Less Options   SVG Code...   ⊕   OK   Cancel

Figure 1-20. *SVG Options dialog box lower buttons*

The globe icon allows you to preview the image in a browser. However, at this point, you would not have added any additional interactivity. Click OK if you want to save the file as an SVG (.svg) or SVG compressed (.svgz), or click Cancel and exit the dialog box.

Option 2: File ➤ Export ➤ Export for Screens (For Multiple File formats)

Besides using File ➤ Export ➤ Export As which after clicking export reveals this dialog box, as in Figure 1-21.

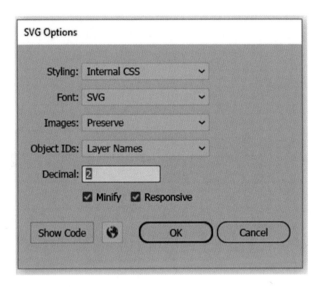

Figure 1-21. *SVG Options dialog box*

Illustrator has another way to export your web files, known as Export for Screens, as seen here in Figure 1-22.

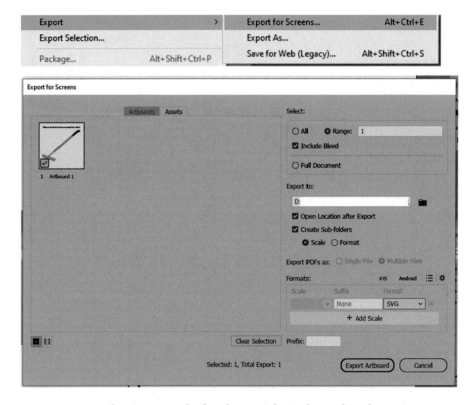

Figure 1-22. Export for Screens dialog box with Artboards tab settings

Again, in this case, you would start with an (.ai) or (.eps) file and then choose this option.

The Export for Screens has two tabs for working with your images: Artboards and Assets. Refer to Figure 1-22 and Figure 1-23.

SVG Artboards Tab

In this case, let's look at the Artboards tab first. You can view the selected artboard in a large Thumbnail view or small Thumbnail view or clear the selection. This is similar to what we have been working with when you need to File Save ➤ As a document; however, when you use Export for Screens, you can save in other file formats at the same time. Refer to Figure 1-23.

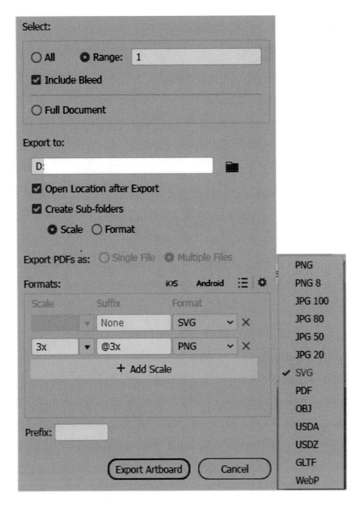

Figure 1-23. *Export for Screens dialog box Assets settings*

Note that some of the formats may not be available to you if you are not working on 3D- related files.

If there are multiple artboards, you can set All or a Range; Include Bleed is checked by default, or instead, set it to Full Document. The Artboards can be exported to specific folder locations and subfolders based on scale or format. You can export as PDF if that is a file format selected as a single or multiple files, as well as adjust the Formats scale, suffix ending, and prefix beginning for various formats.

In the Formats area are several buttons, to the right of iOS, Android device presents and "settings for exported preset" list icon, and when you click the gear icon presents an "Advanced settings for exported file types." This icon will allow you to set your exported artboards with correct SVG settings. Refer to Figure 1-24.

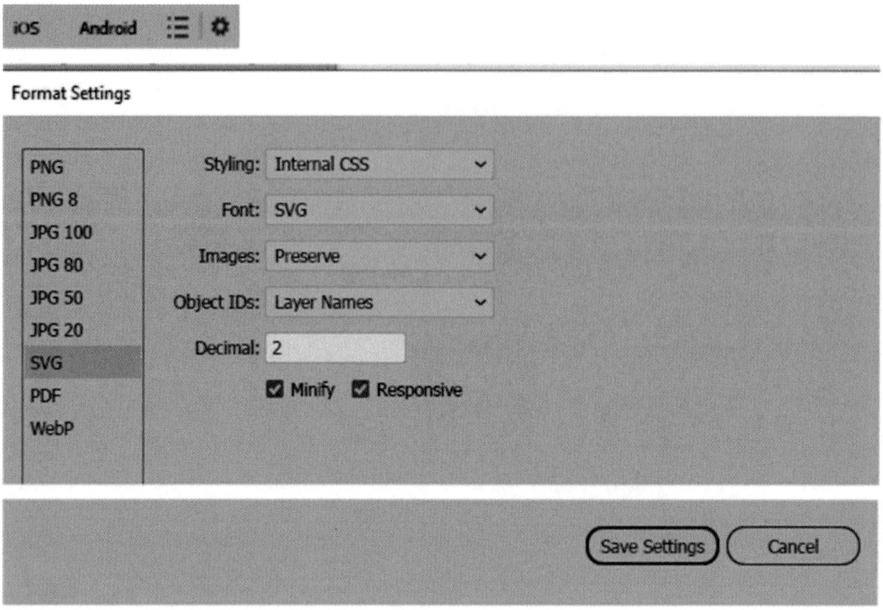

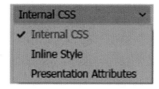

Figure 1-24. *Advanced Format Settings for SVG in the Format Settings dialog box*

In this dialog box, called Format Settings, you can see many of the similar settings that are available when in Option 1 you used File ➤ Save As and saved as an SVG and for Export As here in the section "Option 2." Refer to this section and "Option 1" for clarification, but note that they have been arranged in a slightly different order in the Format Settings dialog box.

You can adjust how the SVG is internally styled. Internal CSS is the default, but you can choose Inline Style or Presentation Attributes. Refer to Figure 1-25.

Figure 1-25. *Advanced Format Settings for SVG for Styling*

These are the Font (Convert to Outlines and SVG) and Images (Preserve, Embed, and Link) lists options. Refer to Figure 1-26.

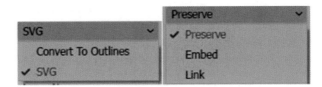

Figure 1-26. *Advanced Format Settings for SVG for Font and Image*

The Internal Object IDs, by default, are set to Layer Names. Other Options are Minimal and Unique. Refer to Figure 1-27.

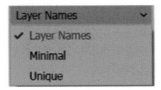

Figure 1-27. *Advanced Format Settings for SVG, Object IDs*

The precision of the vectors (Decimal) (0–15) the default is 2, compression (Minify) is enabled Responsive when enabled allows the CSS to make the SVG image scalable in the browser. Refer to Figure 1-28.

Figure 1-28. *Advanced Format Settings for SVG, Decimal, Minify, and Responsive*

Note   If any of these items in the Format Settings dialog box for SVG Tab are unfamiliar to you, you can hover over them with your mouse to get a hint as in Figure 1-29.

Figure 1-29. *Hover over a field in the dialog box to get a hint*

You can save these settings or click Cancel to exit. Refer to Figure 1-30.

Figure 1-30. *Save Settings and Cancel button in the Format Settings dialog box*

SVG Assets Tab

The Assets tab has basically the same settings as the Artboards tab; however, this is best for when you select actual grouped paths and shapes (artwork) on the Artboard. We will look at a better way to use this area via the Asset Export panel at the end of the chapter and discuss it further in Chapter 3. Refer to the section "SVG Artboards Tab" if you need to review some of the settings and options discussed so far. Refer to Figure 1-31.

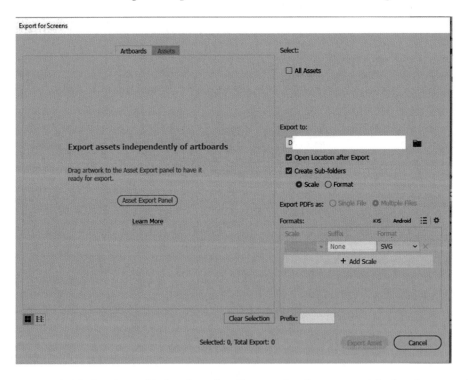

Figure 1-31. *SVG Options dialog box for Export for Screens with the Assets tab*

Remember: If any setting is unfamiliar to you, you can hover over a word for a hint.

Exporting an SVG File (Tool Project Example)

Earlier in the chapter, you looked at SVG Interactivity to create a graphic that when the mouse hovered over, it would change color or when clicked on, an alert message would appear. For HTML pages, the client will sometimes want a shape to have some information appear when hovering over a part rather than an alert message. With SVG Interactivity, you can create a type of informational guide or map so that when you hover over part of an illustration or shape, a message could appear. File ➤ Open the file Parts_ of_a_rake.ai file in this chapter's folder for reference. Later, we will open the Parts_of_a_ rake_2.svg file in your browser and see how it interacts, as in Figure 1-32.

Hover over part of the Rake to discover what that part is called.

Hilt

Figure 1-32. *When you hover over the parts of a tool, you can determine what each piece is called*

When you hover over each part of the rake, you can discover what the name of that part is. This technique could be very useful for your own project where you might want information on distinct parts of a map or tool to guide people. Other examples could be parts of an organ like an ear or eye or distinct parts of a flower. There are many possibilities. I will show you a few more examples as we progress through the chapter.

Here is how it works, in the file Parts_of_a_rake.ai. I have created below the Target layer nine sublayers and named them. Four of them are the parts of the rake in grayscale color (Head, Handle, Shaft, Hilt). Note that the head is grouped as it has several paths. The Title layer is just the sentence and is not part of the interactivity. The other four layers are the grouped text messages along with a color version of that part (HeadLink, HiltLink, HandleLink, ShaftLink). They will eventually be, once in SVG format, linked to that part of the rake so that they can be turned on and off when a hover over that part takes place. Refer to the Layers panel and Figures 1-33 and 1-34.

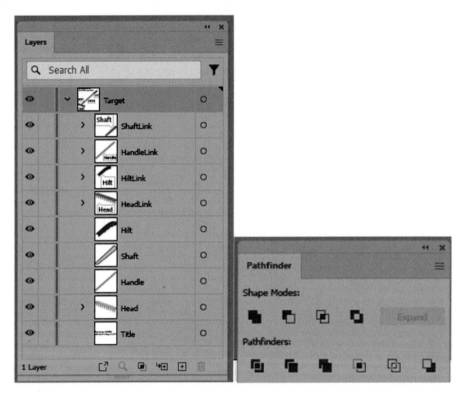

Figure 1-33. *The Layers panel with each sublayer name and how it is organized and Pathfinder panel used to modify some paths*

Layer order with these kinds of projects is very important, as well as the design of parts, as you want to avoid clutter or unnecessary parts showing and hiding when you hover. You will discover this as you build your own projects and find out that sometimes the overlay shape may need to be modified and the paths adjusted to work with the design. If you use the exact shapes to overlay, they may incorrectly overlap when you hover.

Tip   Use your Pathfinder panel for modifying some shapes as mentioned in Volume 1. Refer to Figure 1-33 if you need to locate that panel.

Right now, Figure 1-34 looks a bit cluttered on the Artboard, but we will change that shortly.

Figure 1-34. *How the sublayers currently appear on the Artboard*

When I named my layers or sublayers, I gave them single one-word names, and I made sure that I clearly knew which text link would go with what part of the tool. When you choose longer names, you can write them either with letters or numbers (object1, object2) or with what scripter's call Camel Code (HandleLink, ShaftLink) where one or more letters may be capitalized so that you see a break in the word. Avoid using dashes (-), underscores (_), or spaces in your names as this will cause the SVG Interactivity links to fail.

Once you have reviewed the file, leave the layers as you see them in Figure 1-33. And Choose File ➤ Save As or File ➤ Save A Copy (if you want the original AI file to remain open while working on the SVG file) and choose to save as an SVG. Save your file as Parts_of_a_rake_JH.svg (use your initials) so you do not overwrite my example Parts_of_a_rake_2.svg. Click Save. Refer to Figure 1-35.

Figure 1-35. *Save your file as an SVG*

Now choose the following SVG Options settings. Refer to Figure 1-36.

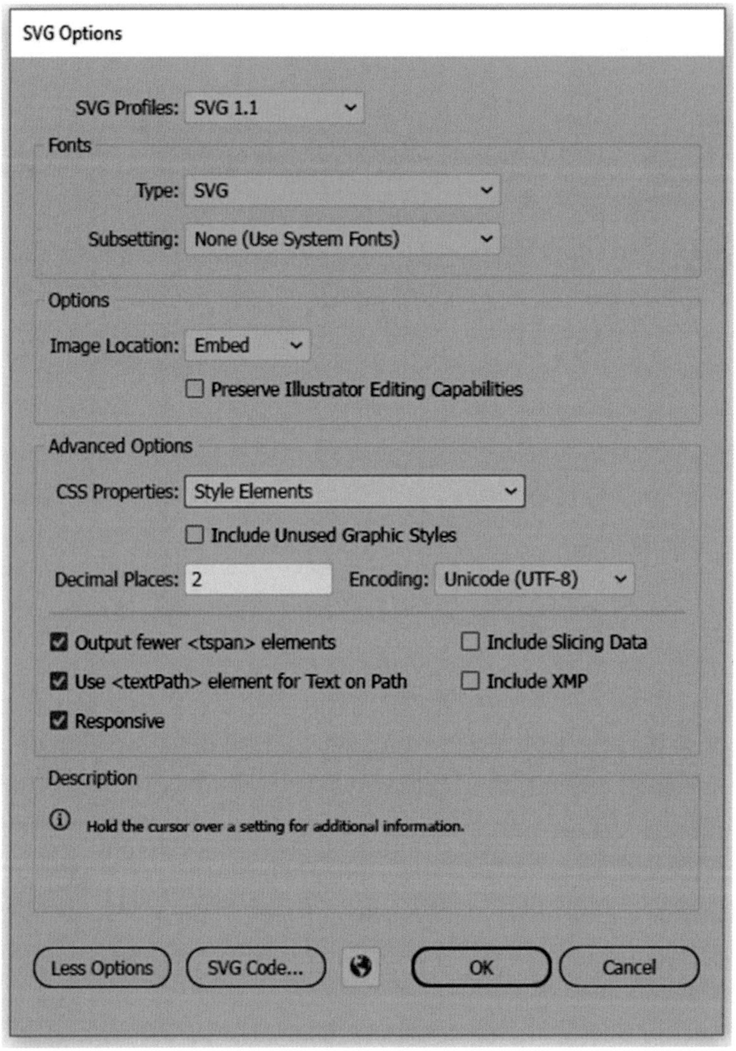

Figure 1-36. *Settings in the SVG Options dialog box*

SVG Profiles: SVG 1.1

Type: SVG

Subsetting: None (Use System fonts)

Image Location: Embed

Unchecked: Preserve Illustrator Editing Capabilities

CSS Properties: Style Elements

Unchecked: Include Unused Graphic Styles

Decimal Places: 2 Encoding: Unicode (UTF-8)

Check: Output fewer <tspan> elements,

Check: Use <textPath> element for Text on a Path

Check: Responsive

Leave the other two settings (Include Slicing Data and Include XMP) unchecked.

When done, click OK to save your file.

If the newly created SVG file Parts_of_a_rake_JH.svg is not in Illustrator, choose File ➤ Open and locate the file. You can also open the file Parts_of_a_rake_2.svg if you want to compare the code that you will enter.

You can close my original AI file Parts_of_a_rake.ai without saving changes. However, for your own (.ai) file, make sure that you File ➤ Save your work before closing it.

Now in the SVG file, look again at the Layers panel. They should look the same as what you saw in the AI file. Refer to Figure 1-37.

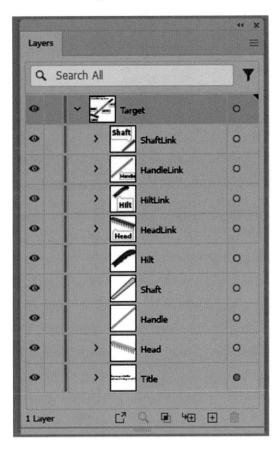

Figure 1-37. *The Layers panel as viewed in the SVG File*

Now turn off all the visibility eyes for the four sublayers with the word "Link" in them so that the information boxes are no longer visible, as in Figure 1-38. Now the Artboard is less cluttered. Keep the main Target layer eye on.

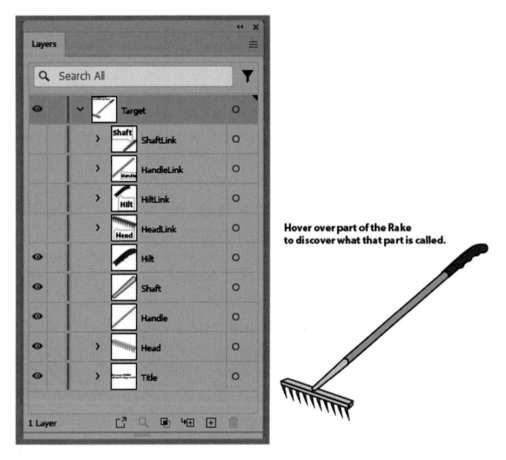

Figure 1-38. *The text link layers visibility is turned off, and the Artboard appears less cluttered*

If you do notice on your own project that a sublayer has become ungrouped during conversion, such as the Title, you can, at this point, select both layer circle targets (Shift+click) and Choose Object ➤ Group, and then rename the group (double-click) and retype back to Title or whatever the original was called. Refer to Figure 1-39.

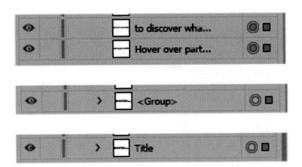

Figure 1-39. *In the SVG file, you can group layers if they became ungrouped and rename*

Make sure to File ➤ Save the SVG file at this point.

Note   As we saw earlier in the chapter, the AI file when converted to an SVG does not always retain the JavaScript. If you enter it into the SVG Interactivity panel, save the file as an SVG, and then open the SVG. For my workflow, I find it better to enter the JavaScript only into the SVG file. That way if I need to use the original AI file for other projects, it keeps the object's shapes clean of extra code which might be accidentally copied into other AI files. Also, sometimes filters may not always convert correctly in the SVG file, so you may need to alter your graphics slightly if certain colors don't convert as expected.

In the Layers panel, select the sublayer called "Hilt," and click select the circle target on the right so that you know this object is fully selected. Refer to Figure 1-40.

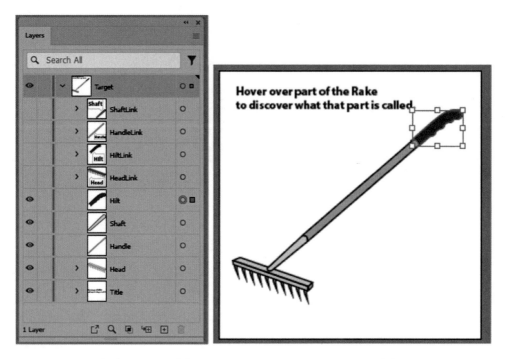

Figure 1-40. *With the Hilt sublayer targeted, you can now add SVG Interactivity to the object*

Now go to the Window ➤ SVG Interactivity panel.

While the target is selected, choose Event "onmouseover" from the drop-down and enter the following code into the JavaScript box as in Figure 1-41:

```
document.getElementById("HiltLink").style.display="block";
```

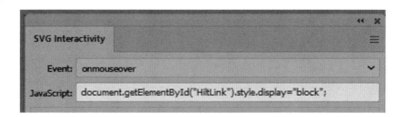

Figure 1-41. *Add your JavaScript code for an object to the SVG Interactivity panel*

Click into the lower box area to confirm the code, and then choose Event "onmouseout" and type the following code into the JavaScript area, as in Figure 1-42:

```
document.getElementById("HiltLink").style.display="none";
```

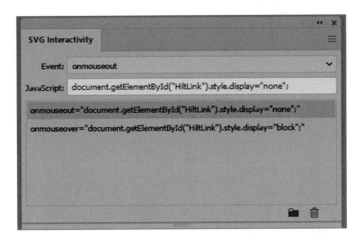

Figure 1-42. *Add your JavaScript code for an object to the SVG Interactivity panel*

Click in the lower gray area to confirm it into the SVG Interactivity panel, and save your SVG file.

As earlier in the chapter, when you changed the object's color to show or hide, here you have set the "HiltLink" text to show when the mouse hovers over the object "block." To hide, it is set to "none" when the mouse moves away from the object.

After Saving the file, try this file in your browser, and you will see when you hover over or move away from the Hilt shape that the text shows and hides and the hilt changes color. Refer to Figure 1-43.

Figure 1-43. *In the browser, when you hover over the hilt, a message will appear, and it will hide when you move away from the object*

You will now want to create interactivity for all the other parts of the rake. If you get confused, you can refer to my file Parts_of_a_rake_2.svg.

However, make sure that for each object, always select the layer and the target circle for that layer so that the entire part is selected. Refer to Figure 1-44.

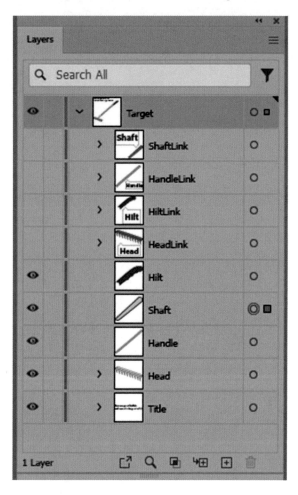

Figure 1-44. *In the Layers panel, always select the target for a layer so that it will be linked correctly in the SVG Interactivity panel*

Only then should you start adding your JavaScript to the SVG Interactivity panel. Here is a table of the remaining code. Refer to Table 1-1.

Table 1-1. *The remaining code for each sublayer*

Target Color	Event	JavaScript
Shaft	onmouseover	document.getElementById("ShaftLink").style.display="block";
	onmouseout	document.getElementById("ShaftLink").style.display="none";
Handle	onmouseover	document.getElementById("HandleLink").style.display="block";
	onmouseout	document.getElementById("HandleLink").style.display="none";
Head	onmouseover	document.getElementById("HeadLink").style.display="block";
	onmouseout	document.getElementById("HeadLink").style.display="none";

Once you have entered the code, make sure to save your file and test it in the browser. You may have to go back to Illustrator to make changes to the SVG and save and then refresh the browser.

As you can see, you don't have to know a lot of JavaScript to find creative ways to work with Illustrator's SVG Interactivity panel.

Note   For your own project, if it has a lot of sublayers, if you find that some shapes are still not disappearing initially when the file opens in the browser and only disappear after being hovered over once, make sure to check your layer order in the SVG. Sometimes certain upper sublayers eyes need to remain on, while lower sublayers eyes need to be turned off, as in Figure 1-45. Again, this all has to do with how you decide to organize your layer order.

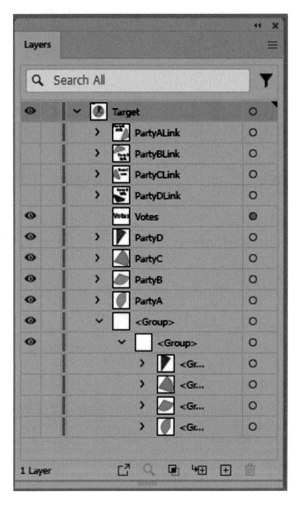

Figure 1-45. *Check your layer order if you notice that your SVG file does not respond correctly in the browser*

Project Idea: Pie Graph Example

You could take this same idea and coding as well to create an interactive pie graph example. You can see that in the files Graph_parts.ai and Graph_parts.svg. Refer to Figure 1-46.

In a (.ai) file, you can start with a pie graph, as you created in Volume 2, and then create a copy of the layer (drag the layer over the create new layer icon). Turn that copy into an Object ➤ Ungroup(ed) file so that it is no longer a graph, and modify those shapes. Add additional grouped sublayers with type and markers. Lock and turn off your original <graph> layer; if you do not want it to be modified, then only edit your copied paths. Refer to Figure 1-46.

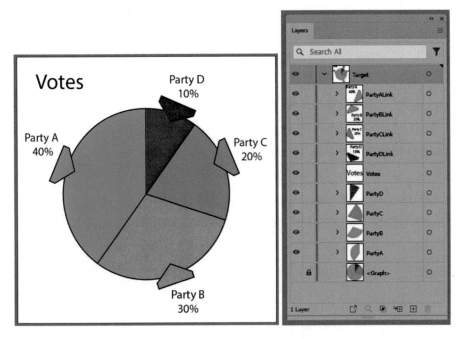

Figure 1-46. *Create a SVG graph using a pie graph and the Layers panel*

After you save the file as an SVG, as mentioned in the steps earlier, you will notice that your original graph will turn into a grouped layer as SVGs do not retain graph information, and you can turn that layer off if you do not want it as part of the project. You can also, as you did earlier, hide the sublayer that you will want to reveal later when hovered over. Refer to Figure 1-47.

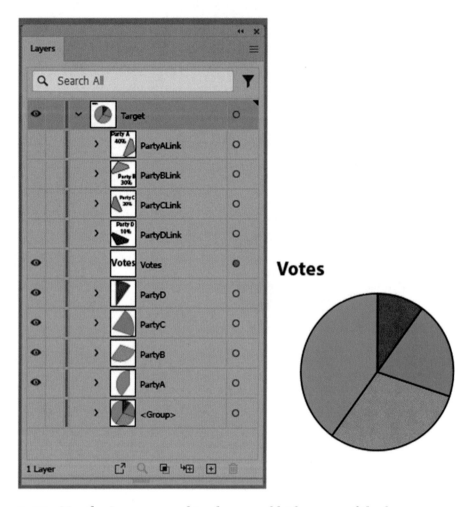

Figure 1-47. *Use the Layers panel to show and hide some of the layers*

Again, you can then target a wedge shape and then use the SVG Interactivity panel to trigger the events and add JavaScript for a specific sublayer, in this case, the sublayer "PartDLink," that onmouseout you want to set to "none" (hide), and for onmouseover you want to set to "block" (show). Refer to Figure 1-47 and Figure 1-48.

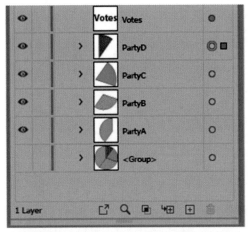

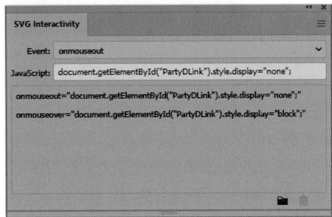

Figure 1-48. *Select your Target layer item before you enter the SVG Interactivity panel*

Save your file and view it in the browser and test. In this SVG example, you can hover over other wedges to see different information. Refer to Figure 1-49.

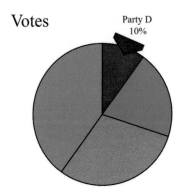

Figure 1-49. *Interactive SVG graph*

Displaying an SVG Infographic online

SVG Images are meant for displaying online as part of a web page. While you can test them and scale them in the browser, when you want to display them with additional information on a web page, you need to design the page first in an HTML editor, like Notepad++ or Adobe Dreamweaver.

Note that if you have not used Dreamweaver before, you can just follow along with my notes and refer to my code. The purpose of this book is not to describe all the HTML options since you can learn more about this from my mentioned book at the beginning of the chapter and some tutorial resources that I will provide at the end of this section. The main thing in this chapter is to understand where and how an SVG file can be placed within the code of a basic HTML page.

As mentioned, I'll just demonstrate the code in Dreamweaver, but on your own, you can type and edit or open the files using Notepad++ if you prefer. In this example, refer to the SVG_WebPage folder in your chapter's project folder and use Dreamweaver to File ➤ Open the file index.html to view how the SVG can be linked on a very basic web page.

Project: After Adding Interactivity to an SVG File, Try Saving the Graphic on a Basic HTML Page

At this point, make sure that you have downloaded Dreamweaver from the Creative Cloud Desktop, as mentioned in the Introduction. Refer to Figure 1-50.

Figure 1-50. *Use the Creative Cloud Desktop to open Dreamweaver if it is installed*

Working with SVG Images in Dreamweaver

In Dreamweaver, I earlier create my own file using File ➤ New in the New Document dialog box I set, Document Type: HTML page. I gave it a Title, and I am using the Doc Type of HTML5. I left the Attach CSS area blank and clicked the Create button. Refer to Figure 1-51.

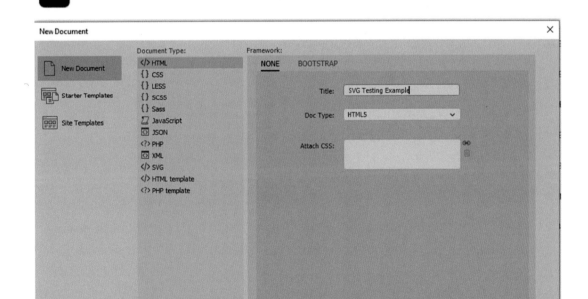

Figure 1-51. *Create a new HTML document using Dreamweaver New Document dialog box*

Later I added my SVG files as well as some internal CSS (cascading style sheet) code.

Internal CSS in this example is not required for the SVG file to be inserted, but adding a border around the image in this case can help you see its boundaries better in the browser for the purpose of displaying and testing my example. Refer to Figure 1-52.

```
 1  <!doctype html>
 2 ▼ <html lang="en">
 3 ▼ <head>
 4    <meta charset="utf-8">
 5    <title>SVG Testing Example</title>
 6 ▼ <style type="text/css">
 7 ▼     .sizing{
 8            border-color: black;
 9            border-width: 2px;
10            border-style: solid;
11            width: 500px;
12            height: 500px;
13        }
14 ▼     .sizing2{
15            border-color: black;
16            border-width: 2px;
17            border-style: solid;
18            width: 50%;
19            height: 50%;
20        }
21    </style>
22    </head>
23
24 ▶  <body> <h1>SVG file displa...
35    </html>
36
```

Figure 1-52. *Internal CSS was added to this HTML page*

I view my code and the changes using Split view Live so that I can see basic changes rather than have the browser open at the same time. However, afterward, you should view the page in the browser as well to review any changes you make. This figure shows the standard Dreamweaver workspace. Refer to Figure 1-53.

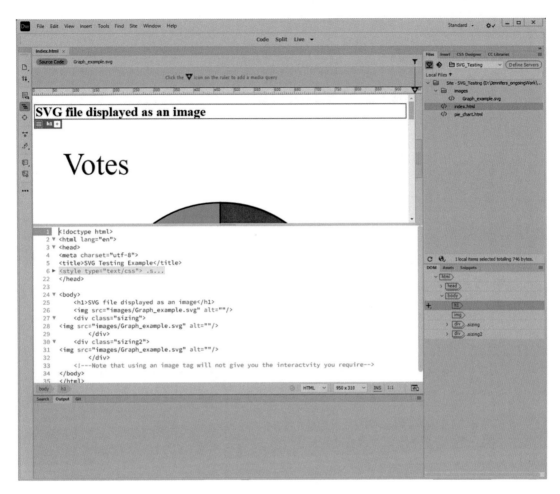

Figure 1-53. *Dreamweaver standard workspace*

Also, I sent up in my Files panel with a new local folder site using Site ➤ New Site from the main menu and saved my the Site Setup dialog box options, so that I can access my index.html and other HTML pages easily using my Files panel. Refer to Figures 1-54 and 1-55.

Site Setup for Unnamed Site 2   ✕

Site
Servers
> CSS Preprocessors
> Advanced Settings

A Dreamweaver site is a collection of all of the files and assets you use in your website. A Dreamweaver site usually has two parts: a local folder on your computer where you store and work on files, and a remote folder on a server where you post the same files to the web.

Here you'll select the local folder and a name for your Dreamweaver site.

Site Name: Unnamed Site 2

Local Site Folder: D:\

Help   Cancel   Save

Figure 1-54. Setting up a local site for testing using Dreamweaver's Site Setup dialog box

Give your site a name such as "SVG_Testing," locate the local site folder you are building the website in, select the folder, and click Save to exit the Site Setup dialog box. Refer to Figures 1-54 and 1-55.

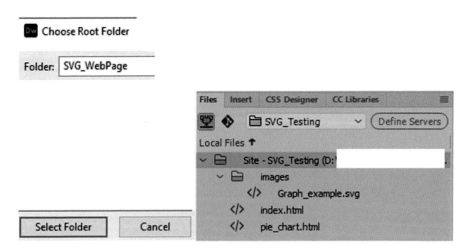

Figure 1-55. Set up and manage your site using Dreamweaver and display in the Files panel

The links can be viewed in your Dreamweaver Files panel as Local Files as we are not building a remote website.

Tip   Use Site ➤ Manage Sites if you need to edit your Site setting at a later time.

You can learn more about basic site setup and how to build basic web pages from the following Adobe links that I will provide at the end of this section.

If you File ➤ Open an SVG file directly in Dreamweaver, you would see the following code, and this can run on for many lines, based on the complexity of the file. Refer to Figure 1-56.

```
index.html*  ×    Graph_example.svg  ×
 1   <?xml version="1.0" encoding="utf-8"?>
 2   <!-- Generator: Adobe Illustrator 27.8.1, SVG Export Plug-In . SVG Version: 6.00 Build 0)  -->
 3 ▼ <svg version="1.1" id="Target" xmlns="http://www.w3.org/2000/svg" xmlns:xlink="http://www.w3.org/1999/xlink" x="0px" y="0px"
 4       viewBox="0 0 270 270" style="enable-background:new 0 0 270 270;" xml:space="preserve">
 5 ▼ <style type="text/css">
 6       .st0{display:none;}
 7       .st1{display:inline;}
 8       .st2{fill:#00AEEF;stroke:#000000;stroke-width:0.5;stroke-miterlimit:10;}
 9       .st3{fill:#F7941D;stroke:#000000;stroke-width:0.5;stroke-miterlimit:10;}
10       .st4{fill:#00A651;stroke:#000000;stroke-width:0.5;stroke-miterlimit:10;}
11       .st5{fill:#EF4136;stroke:#000000;stroke-width:0.5;stroke-miterlimit:10;}
12       .st6{fill:#00AEEF;stroke:#000000;stroke-miterlimit:10;}
13       .st7{fill:#F7941D;stroke:#000000;stroke-miterlimit:10;}
14       .st8{fill:#00A651;stroke:#000000;stroke-miterlimit:10;}
15       .st9{fill:#EF4136;stroke:#000000;stroke-miterlimit:10;}
16       .st10{fill:#231F20;}
17       .st11{font-family:'MyriadPro-Bold';}
18       .st12{font-size:22px;}
19       .st13{display:inline;fill:#231F20;}
20       .st14{font-size:12px;}
21       .st15{display:inline;fill:#ED1C24;stroke:#231F20;stroke-miterlimit:10;}
22       .st16{display:inline;fill:#00A651;stroke:#231F20;stroke-miterlimit:10;}
23       .st17{display:inline;fill:#F7941D;stroke:#231F20;stroke-miterlimit:10;}
24       .st18{display:inline;fill:#00AEEF;stroke:#231F20;stroke-miterlimit:10;}
25   </style>
26 ▼ <g class="st0">
```

Figure 1-56. *How the code appears for an SVG file in Dreamweaver*

In the case of SVG files, directly created from Illustrator, due to their length, I would not recommend copying and pasting this into the Dreamweaver code area. Instead, it is better to first try an image tag <img/> if you want to insert the file into your code.

In this case, you can click somewhere between the <body> opening and </body> closing tag of your HTML file, and from your main menu, choose Insert ➤ Image or use the Insert panel on the HTML setting to do the same. Locate your file in the images folder, in this case, the file Graph_example.svg, and click OK. Refer to Figure 1-57.

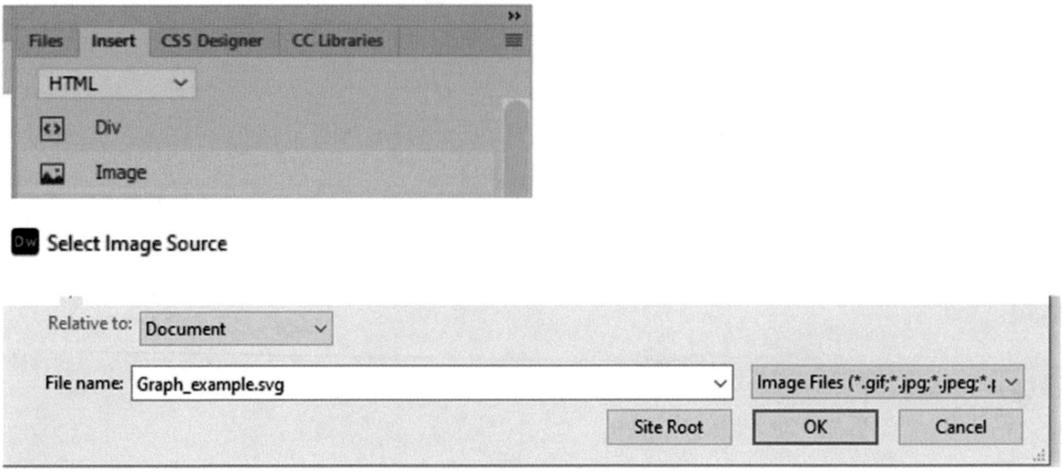

Figure 1-57. *Use the Dreamweaver Insert panel to locate and place a link to the SVG file*

This is the code that appears:

```
<img src="images/Graph_example.svg" alt=""/>
```

Note   Your link location (src) may vary if you have not set up a root folder as I did. Refer to the links mentioned at the end of this section on how to do that.

When you insert an SVG file as an image, you will not see a width or height attribute as you would with PNG, GIF, or JPEG images when you use the <img/> tag. These are left empty, as seen, if you refer to the Widow ➤ Properties panel. Refer to Figure 1-58.

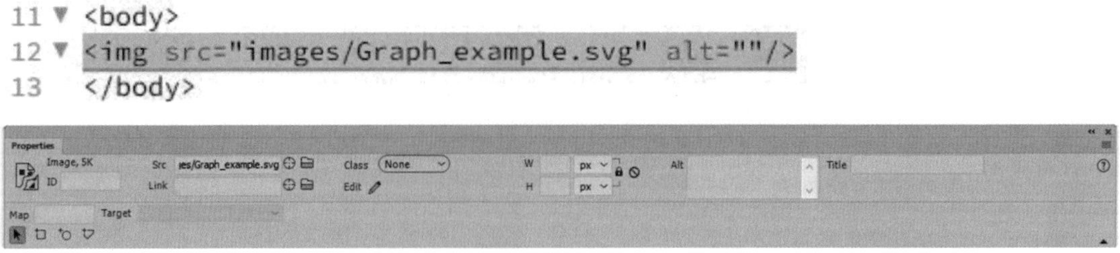

```
11 ▼  <body>
12 ▼  <img src="images/Graph_example.svg" alt=""/>
13     </body>
```

Figure 1-58. *HTML code for image link and Dreamweaver's Properties panel*

SVG or Scalable Vector Graphics are meant to size to whatever area they are placed into without losing quality. If you have used the setting of Responsive within the SVG, then your image will be able to scale up or down to fill an area on your page. You cannot simply insert an SVG image on a page and expect it to display at a set-scaled size without adjusting the code.

To view the SVG, while you are editing in Dreamweaver, make sure you're in Live view, not Design view; otherwise, it appears as a broken image icon on the page. Refer to Figure 1-14 for responsive setting. Refer to Figure 1-58 and Figure 1-59 for referene to broken link icon.

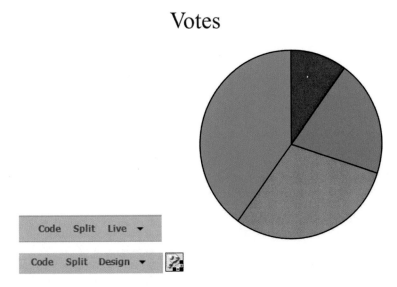

Figure 1-59. *An SVG appears as a broken image in Design view on a web page; in live view, the graph is visible*

Note   If you plan to insert your SVG file into an HTML file, be aware that if you insert it as an image <img/> tag, the graphic will appear, and it will be responsive, but the interactivity will be unavailable. SVG, while it appears as an image, is more of a set of codes and coordinates simply projecting an image. To keep the interactivity of the SVG, you need to copy the code of that file, including the actions, into the HTML file itself or use an <object> tag instead. You can see that in my example, in a moment. When an SVG is in an <img/> tag, you can force the image to size using CSS and adjusting the width and height. This can get complicated, so we'll look at this issue in more detail now.

A better way to work with an SVG is to insert into a <div></div> tag so that you can scale the width and height of the <div> with CSS. You can refer to my index.html file to see how this was done for various examples, using CSS classes. However, this will still not correct the interactivity issue. Refer to Figure 1-60.

```
 6 ▼ <style type="text/css">
 7 ▼     .sizing{
 8           border-color: black;
 9           border-width: 2px;
10           border-style: solid;
11           width: 500px;
12           height: 500px;
13       }
14 ▼     .sizing2{
15           border-color: black;
16           border-width: 2px;
17           border-style: solid;
18           width: 50%;
19           height: 50%;
20       }
21   </style>
22   </head>
23
24 ▼ <body>
25       <h1>SVG file displayed as an image</h1>
26       <img src="images/Graph_example.svg" alt=""/>
27 ▼     <div class="sizing">
28   <img src="images/Graph_example.svg" alt=""/>
29           </div>
30 ▼     <div class="sizing2">
31   <img src="images/Graph_example.svg" alt=""/>
32           </div>
```

Figure 1-60. *Examples of CSS coding to alter the size of an image tag*

The best option is to wrap it within an <object> </object> tag, as you can see on the pie_chart.html page in Live view.

The code that I used in that case was as follows:

```
<object id="EdgeID2" type="text/html" width="500" height="500" data-dw-
widget="Edge" data="images/Graph_example.svg"></object>
```

50

The <object> tag allows you to keep the interactivity of the SVG as well as you can apply CSS to adjust scaling. If you want to keep the responsiveness rather than using actual pixel numbers, use percentages instead:

```
<object id="EdgeID2" type="text/html" width="50%" height="50%" data-dw-
widget="Edge" data="images/Graph_example.svg"></object>
```

Either way, adding width and height will constrain how much the object can scale, but with percentage, it will still slightly scale and be responsive if the browser changes size as well.

If you have more than one SVG on the page, make sure to give each a unique identifier or ID like this:

```
<object id="EdgeID1" type="text/html" width="500" height="500" data-dw-
widget="Edge" data="images/Graph_example.svg"></object>
        <object id="EdgeID2" type="text/html" width="50%" height="50%" data-
        dw-widget="Edge" data="images/Graph_example.svg"></object>
```

Note   The object tag can also be used when you insert an OAM (Animated Composition) for the HTML5 canvas that was created using Adobe Animate. I will mention Animate briefly in Chapter 3.

Two other additional tag methods you could try using are <embed> which creates a container for external applications or plug-in content and <iframe></iframe> which creates an inline frame. Both of these will allow you to keep your interactivity of your SVG. However, the iframe may require CSS to make it responsive. You can see the code here:

```
<embed src="images/Graph_example.svg">
<iframe src="images/Graph_example.svg"></iframe>
```

However, for practicing and viewing my graphic, I find the <object> tag to be the most flexible. Remember, if you are not building the website, talk to your web designer about how they will be displaying your graphic and run some tests on the remote site to make sure that it is responsive and displaying the correct interactivity in the browser. Refer to Figure 1-61.

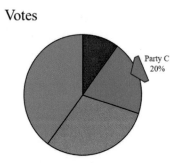

Figure 1-61. *Responsive graph in the browser with added text in HTML page*

Remember to save the file each time in Dreamweaver, before refreshing in your browser, if you want to see the changes.

If you are interested in learning more about basic web layouts and adding additional responsiveness to pages in Dreamweaver, Adobe has some basic tutorials to help you get started. You can also use the Help Menu to access additional tutorials:

- https://helpx.adobe.com/dreamweaver/how-to/make-website-pt1-site-setup.html

- https://helpx.adobe.com/dreamweaver/how-to/make-website-pt2-add-content.html

- https://helpx.adobe.com/dreamweaver/how-to/make-website-pt3-add-html5-elements.html

- https://helpx.adobe.com/dreamweaver/how-to/make-website-pt4-css-design.html

- https://helpx.adobe.com/dreamweaver/how-to/make-website-pt5-css-style.html

- https://helpx.adobe.com/dreamweaver/how-to/make-website-pt6-web-links-navigation.html

- https://helpx.adobe.com/dreamweaver/how-to/make-website-pt7-media-queries-style-sheet.html

- https://helpx.adobe.com/dreamweaver/how-to/make-website-pt8-publish.html

- https://helpx.adobe.com/dreamweaver/tutorials.html?lang=en_US

Another topic related to Dreamweaver and responsiveness that you may want to explore if you are building an actual website to be viewed on mobile devices is the head <meta> tag regarding viewport, device width, and initial scale.

```
<meta name="viewport" content="width=device-width, initial-scale=1">
```

Asset Export Panel and SVG Files in Illustrator

Coming back to Illustrator, rather than using File ➤ Export ➤ Export for Screens and selecting the Assets tab, as you saw earlier in the chapter in the "Option 2" section, another simplified way to export your graphics quickly is to use the Asset Export panel. This can also be used for SVG files as well. Rather than create a large artboard file, you can just drag your artwork into the panel to generate multiple assets or Alt/Option+Drag when you want to generate a single grouped asset when more than one item is selected. Refer to the section "Option 2: File ➤ Export ➤ Export for Screens (For Multiple File formats)" if you need more details on this topic.

You can see here the updated Asset Export panel and its menu with the Export Settings displayed in the following for the various presets and file types. Refer to Figure 1-62.

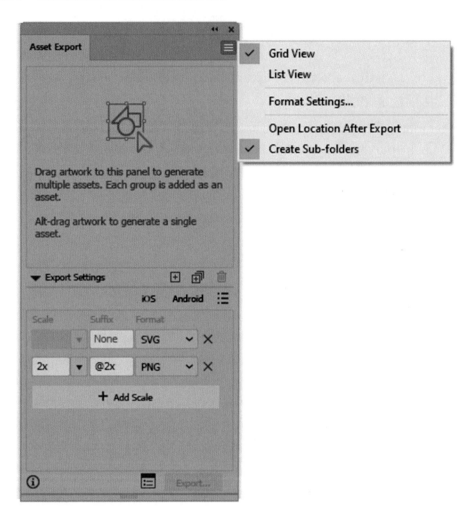

Figure 1-62. *Asset Export panel with menu displayed*

From your own (.ai) file, drag using the Selection tool, a grouped image into the panel from the Artboard, and adjust your file type setting options. You can also, when multiple objects are selected on the Artboard, generate single or multiple assets by clicking that button icon in the panel and later delete/remove them from the Asset Export panel as well while selecting using the trash can icon. Note that this will not remove your artwork from the Artboard. Refer to Figure 1-63.

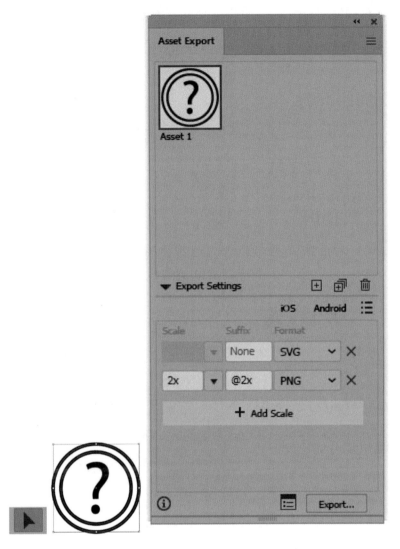

Figure 1-63. *Drag a graphic into the Asset Export panel*

Other web-related files, as mentioned earlier, can include PNG, JPG, PDF, and the new file WebP.

Asset Export, as mentioned in Volume 2 Chapter 5, can also be used for exporting 3D files (OBJ, USDA, USDZ, and GLTF). I'll talk a bit more about Asset Export panel in Chapter 3. However, I will just note that for SVG settings, there will be no scale option in the Export Settings, unlike other scalable formats. Note that if you need to review and access the Export for Screens options, click the list icon at the bottom of the panel, or use your panel's menu if you need to access the Format Settings specifically for SVG. Refer to Figure 1-62.

For more details on SVG, you can refer to the following link:

`https://helpx.adobe.com/illustrator/using/svg.html`

Other Project Ideas

Here are a few more SVG examples using the interactivity code we looked at earlier and applied to some pictures to inform when hovered over.

Parts of a Printing Press

If you wanted to explain the parts of a machine, an SVG file is a great way to do that.

Review the following files: OffestPress_Rollers.ai and OffestPress_Rollers_final.svg. Here we can see the example with all the names and how seeing only one part name at a time would be less cluttered. Refer to Figure 1-64.

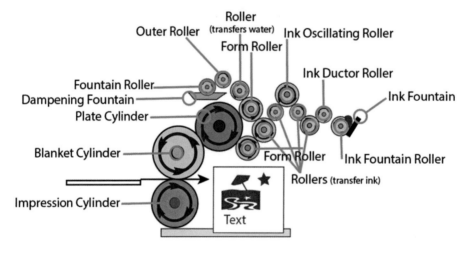

Figure 1-64. *Starting example of the layout for infographic about Offset Press Rollers*

Remember that based on your settings, the SVG font may display as a different font in the browser. I am using a Subsetting of None and relying on the computer's system fonts, so the text may appear instead as Times Roman rather than Myriad Pro.

However, consider also if the infographic is about moving parts. A better idea would be to create an animation in a program like Adobe Animate. We'll talk about that option briefly in Chapter 3.

Under the Sea Levels

Creating an educational infographic for kids, explaining life under the sea and where certain fish are and how deep the ocean is compared to the height of other landmarks, is another interesting project. Refer to files Ocean_Depth.ai and Ocean_Depth_final. svg. In this case, only the sublayers that were interactive were given proper ID names. In the Layers panel, I left nonactive layers at the default names such as <Path> or <Group>. Refer to Figures 1-65 and 1-66.

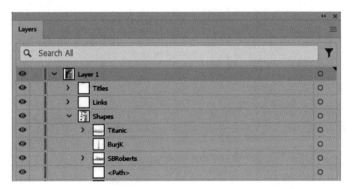

Figure 1-65. *Layers panel, where some layers are renamed and others keep the default name*

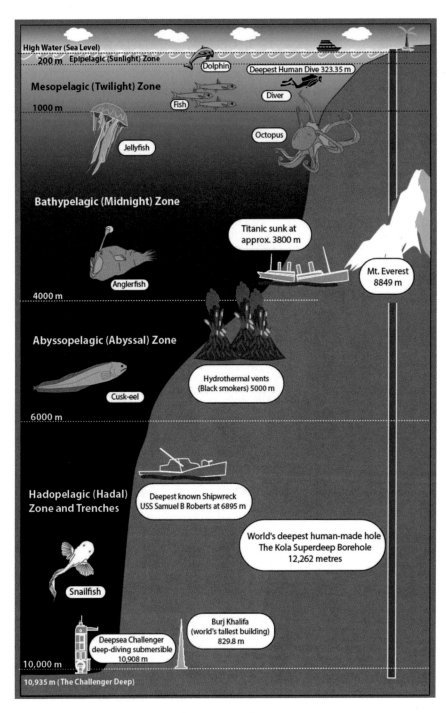

Figure 1-66.   *Ocean layer infographic example*

Again, if you view the SVG in the browser, you will see that this is a good example of how you can hover over an item to show information and then it hides when you move away with "onmouseover" and "onmouseout."

In this case, I added another action to the diver that when I click on him, more information is revealed, and when I click off of him, the information is hidden. This added code was added along with the other code when the Diver layer was targeted to the SVG Interactivity panel. Refer to Figure 1-67.

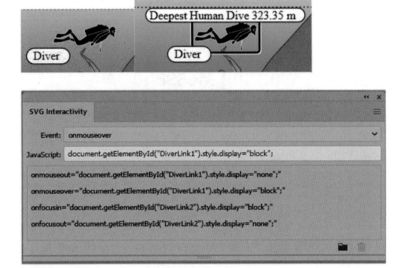

Figure 1-67. *Additional interactivity is added to the diver using the SVG Interactivity panel*

This time I use the Events of onfocusin to show (block) some other text and onfocusout to hide (none) some new information from the element "DiverLink2." "Onfocusin" works when you click on an element, and "onfocusout" is used when you click off the element.

Additionally, besides a title on your own HTML web page, for this kind of project, you would want to add some explanatory text on your web page so that people know that clicking on an item reveals more information in some situations.

On your own, now try to create your own interactive SVG file; it might be a process you want to display such as

- How is flour milled.

- Create a diagram showing the parts of a wheat seed or some other plant.

- Create a simple vendor/exhibitor floor layout where information pops up when you hover over an area. You can see the start of such an idea in Chapter 2.

Correcting an SVG Warning Message

Note that as some SVGs become more complex after you save and close and then open again, in Illustrator, you may get the following warning, "Clipping will be lost on roundtrip to Tiny." Refer to Figure 1-68.

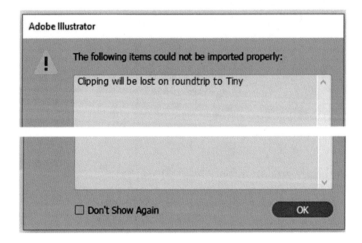

Figure 1-68. *Warning that appears when a clipping mask is present in an SVG file*

In this case, click OK, and view the file for any issue and test in the browser. In most cases, the file should be OK. However, it could be as simple as you used a Symbol in Illustrator and forgot to break the link, and so that layer was left with a clipping mask when it was converted to an SVG. The file should be fine if it is working as it should in the browser, but this is why it is important to always keep a backup copy as an (.ai) file in case you need to make major changes to the artwork. In this case, you can always, in the Layers panel, locate and target select the clip group and choose Object ➤ Clipping Mask ➤ Release. This will release any clipping mask's sublayer in your SVG file. If it is still connected to a Symbol element, then while that symbol is selected, use the Control panel's Break Link button. Leave the group paths as is. Refer to Figures 1-69 and 1-70.

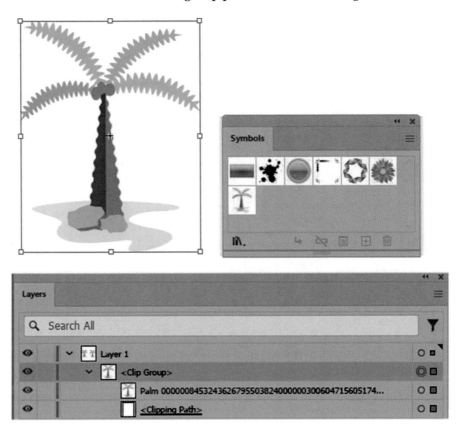

Figure 1-69. *Use the Layers panel to release the clipping path from a selected symbol*

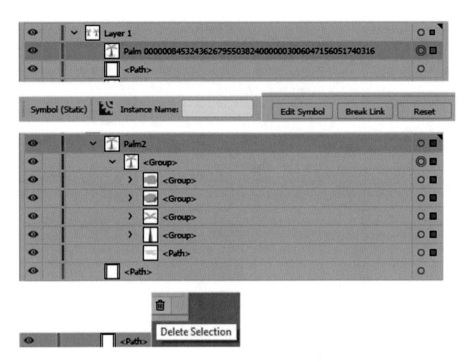

Figure 1-70. *Use the Layers panel and the Control panel to break the link with the Symbol and delete any extra paths*

Likewise, you can always rename the layer if it appears too long because of the symbol conversion and optionally delete any extra path layers that may have been created after the release of the clipping mask or symbol. Refer to Figure 1-70. File ➤ Save your file again. This should remove the error from the SVG.

Likewise, go back to your original file, check for any clipping masks or symbols, and break the link, but leave it as a grouped object before you create an SVG file again.

When you are done, File ➤ Close any open files, and then File ➤ Exit Illustrator or leave open for the next chapter.

You can also File ➤ Close and File ➤ Exit Dreamweaver at this point as we have completed the project for this chapter.

Summary

In this chapter, we reviewed the following on the topic of Scalable Vector Graphics (SVG), how to export assets for screens and the Asset Export panel, and how to add interactivity and display the responsive graphic online in the browser. We also looked at how you can use Dreamweaver to adjust the overall scaling of your SVG file if it is too large.

In the next chapter, we will look at some additional infographic ideas and conclude with thoughts on how to work with your client to complete the infographic as well as design considerations.

Ideas: Various 2D and 3D Graphic Layouts, Client Review

In this chapter, you will be reviewing various infographic examples that you may want to adapt to your own projects.

This chapter will close off our discussion on the process of creating infographics that was started in Volume 1. First, I will show you a few more ideas or topics that you may want to consider or adapt on your own. Then we will conclude the steps that you started in Volume 1 Chapter 2 considering how to review and finish the project with your client when making last-minute modifications as well as learning from feedback.

Note   This chapter does contain project examples that I created which can be found in the Volume 3 Chapter 2 folder.

I will now show you some additional ideas that you may want to try in Illustrator for infographic ideas.

Examples of Various Infographic Layouts

In these examples, I will not go into all the details of the drawing steps, but I will just point out certain highlights from each project that you may want to consider, which appear in either two-dimensional or a combination of two and three dimensions.

© Jennifer Harder 2023
J. Harder, *Creating Infographics with Adobe Illustrator: Volume 3*,
https://doi.org/10.1007/979-8-8688-0038-2_2

Example 1: Exhibitor Floor Plan Layout

As mentioned in Chapter 1, you may need to create a vendor or exhibitor layout that resembles a floor plan. You can view this project in the file FloorLayout.ai. Later, this could be adapted to an SVG layout as well. For now, let us just review the (.ai) file. Refer to Figure 2-1.

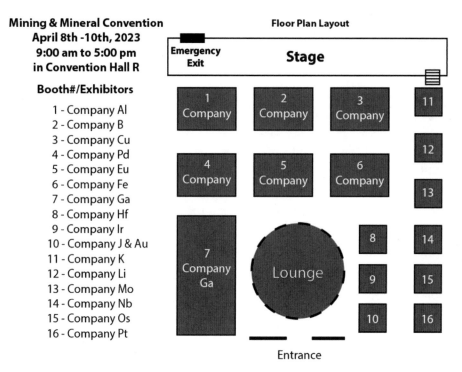

Figure 2-1. *Illustration of a floor plan layout*

These types of layouts can be as simple or complex as you want them to be, and in most cases, they are often a flat two-dimensional layout of the room, displaying areas where the exhibitors will be positioned. These areas are represented by squares, rectangles, and circles. Other basic geometric shapes and lines are used for showing the stage and stairs leading up to the stage, as well as entrances and exits.

The squares are numbered, and if there is enough room in the layout, the name of the exhibitor is put on the square, otherwise it appears in the legend on the right or left-hand side.

In this case, in Illustrator, basic shape tools, type tools, selection tools, the Control, Swatches, and Stroke panels were the main tools and panels used to complete this layout. Refer to Figure 2-2 and Figure 2-3.

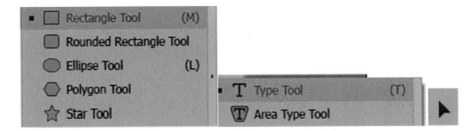

Figure 2-2. *Various shape tools, type tools, and selection tools used for illustration*

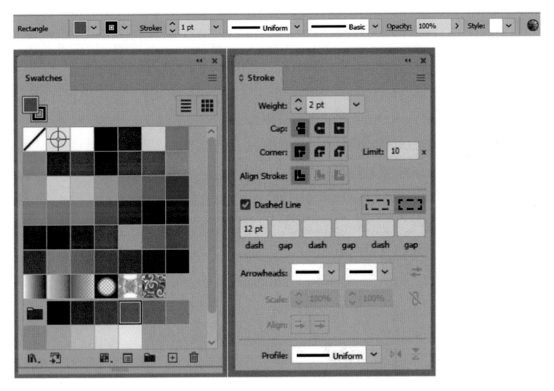

Figure 2-3. *Various panels used for enhancing illustration, Control, Swatches, and Stroke panels*

The Layers panel was also used to keep layers and sublayers organized as the design progressed. I locked and unlocked them to prevent text or images from moving while editing an overlaying object or type. Refer to Figure 2-4.

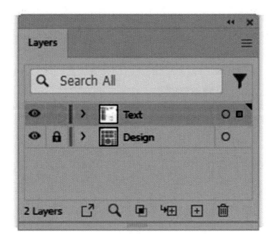

Figure 2-4. *Layers panel with Text layer unlocked and Design layer locked*

Even with a simple infographic like this, there are things to consider when building this design.

Work Timeline

For this project, if it was presented to you by a client with only a few days to complete, then a simple layout like this might be adequate. However, if you had a few months before the event or it was an event held annually in the same location, you may want to add more details such as icons of people or more details about the vendors, which may include logos or additional pictures of some key people.

Amount of Design Space

Detail would of course also depend on how much room on a page you would have to display this infographic. The smaller the design space, the more simplified your layout may have to be. Consult with your client regarding the exact area if the design is to appear in any publication.

Collect Your Information

The next part of the research would be to get an original layout of the floor area from the venue hosting the event. They may already have a floor layout you can use as the background and then build your booth layout over that.

Expect Frequent Changes

Keep in mind that like with creating this kind of infographic, it is subject to frequent changes as the event comes closer to the deadline. Some new exhibitors may appear, or others may drop out at the last moment. As well others may change their location on the layout suddenly. It is important to get the last-minute changes from your client as soon as possible before such a design goes live either in print or online. An online version is easy to correct and can be a relatively inexpensive process, while a reprint takes time and money.

You don't want the audience to be confused when they enter the room only to discover that the Exhibitor is not where they expect them to be.

Practice Your Design Skills

On your own, think about how you could improve this layout for another type of event such as a party, wedding reception, or another corporate event, and create your own layout in Illustrator. What kind of additional pieces of information (text or icons) would you include so that the viewers would easily be able to find the booth or location they needed to visit? Remember when creating a floor layout for an event to answer all or most of the main questions (who, what, when, where, why, and how) using a combination of illustration and text.

Example 2: Recipe Process (Pastry) Page

In this example, I have laid out on an 8.5 ×11 inches artboard the basic recipe process for making pastry. You can view my layout in the file Recipe.ai. Refer to Figure 2-5.

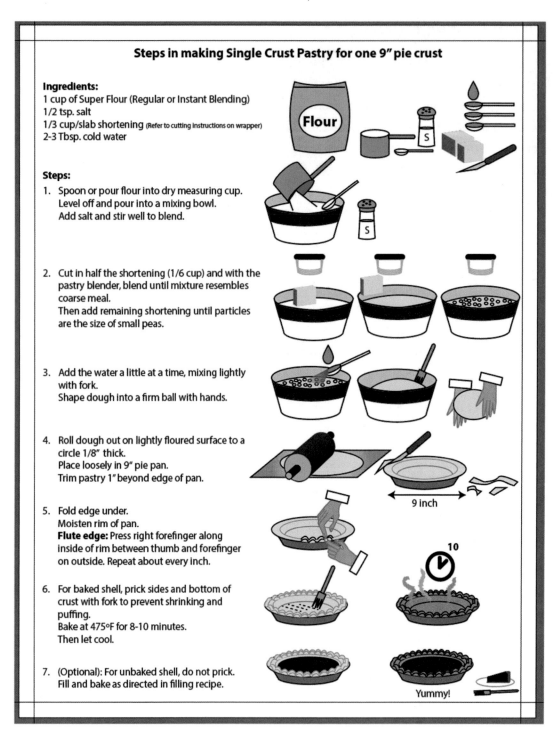

Figure 2-5. *Illustration of the steps for creating a pie crust pastry*

While just text instructions for many recipes are OK, for beginner chefs, a few step-by-step illustrations are always welcome, especially if the student cannot visualize how to do a certain process such as, in this case, fluting the edge of a pastry.

In this case, I used the Type Tool (dragged out a rectangle-type area) and the Control panel to create numbered paragraphs for steps. Refer to Figure 2-6.

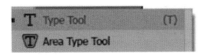

Steps:

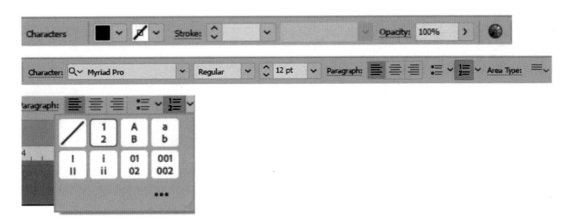

Figure 2-6. *Use the Type Tool and Control panel to create numbered type bullets in a text area*

I also linked several area-type boxes so that I could easily move my text around, depending on the location of the illustration. You can also Shift+click each of your text boxes and use the Align Options in your Control panel when you need, for example, all the left sides to align using Align Left Horizontally. Refer to Figure 2-7.

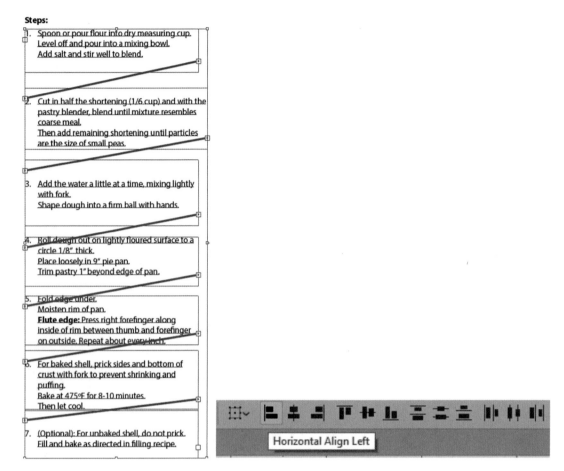

Figure 2-7. *Linked type area can be aligned using the Control panel when they are selected*

The ingredient type area was not linked as I wanted to be able to move this area around and scale it without the text spilling by accident into a linked type area. Refer to Figure 2-8.

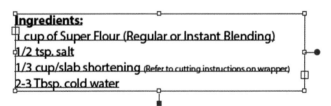

Figure 2-8. *Nonlinked type area*

Note Type area can be linked when you Shift+click each one and then choose Type ➤ Threaded text ➤ Create. You can also release a selection or remove threading. Refer to Figure 2-9.

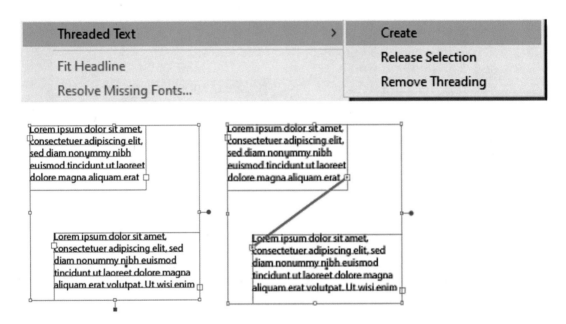

Figure 2-9. *Example of a threaded text area when two selected text boxes are connected*

Likewise, if the type area has too much text, you can click the red plus symbol and then click elsewhere on the Artboard to create a new threaded text area. This was done in the case of the numbered steps. Refer to Figure 2-10.

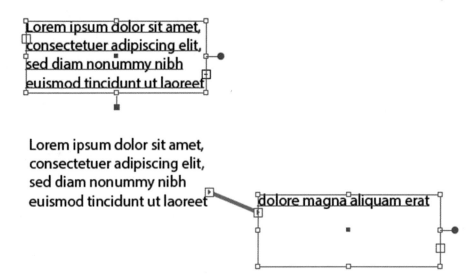

Figure 2-10. *Example of an overflowing type area and threaded text into another area*

In this case, I scaled my text boxes several times so that each numbered step was in its own text area box and used the Shift+Enter/Return keys so that I would get a soft return and not create another number between the substeps. To see your hidden characters, use Type ➤ Show Hidden Characters (Alt/Option+Ctrl/CMD+I) and select again to hide them. Refer to Figure 2-11.

¶
2. Cut·in·half·the·shortening·(1/6·cup)·and·with·the· pastry·blender,·blend·until·mixture·resembles· coarse·meal.·¬
Then·add·remaining·shortening·until·particles· are·the·size·of·small·peas.·¬

2. Cut in half the shortening (1/6 cup) and with the pastry blender, blend until mixture resembles coarse meal.
Then add remaining shortening until particles are the size of small peas.

Figure 2-11. *Text with and without the Show Hidden Characters settings*

The title, in this case, I left as text on Point Type, but you can easily convert it to Area Type or back by selecting it with your Selection Tool using the menu Type ➤ Convert to Area Type or Convert to Point Type as you saw in Volume 1 Chapter 8. Refer to Figure 2-12.

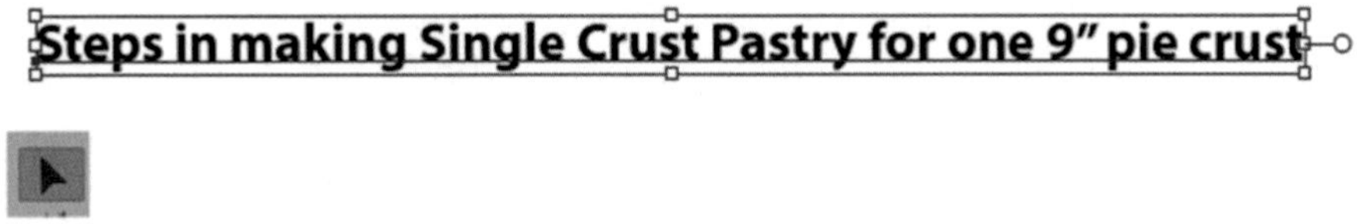

Steps in making Single Crust Pastry for one 9" pie crust

Figure 2-12. *Selected text with Selection Tool*

Once the type and formatting were set, I ran an Edit ➤ Spelling ➤ Check Spelling. In your own project, once the dialog box is open, you would click start and then view the results and choose to Ignore or Change spellings based on suggestions and then click Done when complete. You may want to explore the options area if you need to set different find settings for Repeated Words, Uncapitalized Start of Sentence, or to ignore Words that Are All Uppercase, Roman Numerals, or Words with Numbers. Refer to Figure 2-13.

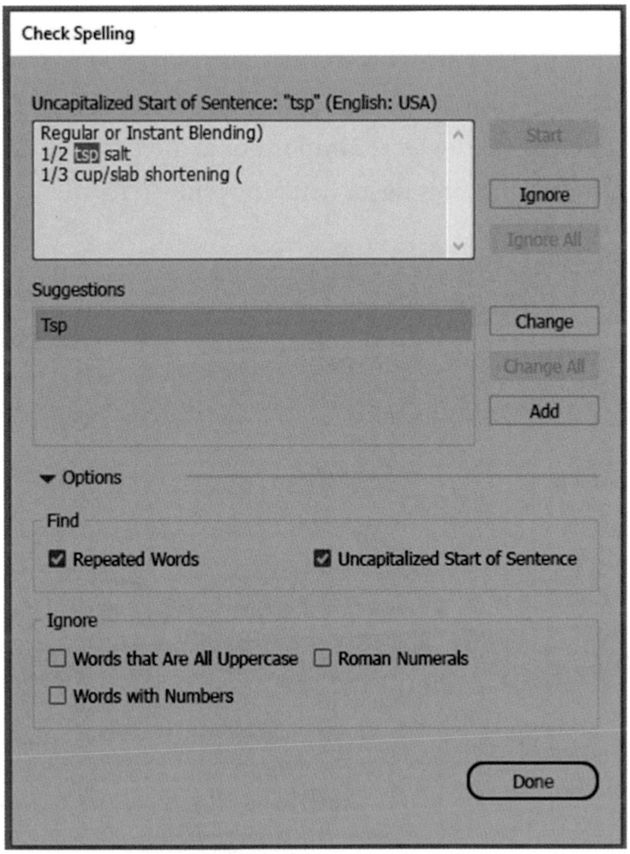

Figure 2-13. *Check Spelling dialog box*

Note   While working on my projects, I will turn off the Edit ➤ Spelling ➤ Auto Spell Check as the red squiggly line can be distracting, but for a last-minute check, always turn it back on to see if there are any errors that you missed. In some cases, you can ignore the line when you purposely type the text a certain way. Refer to Figure 2-14.

Ingredients:
1 cup of Super Flour (Regular or Instant Blending)
1/2 tsp. salt
1/3 cup/slab shortening (Refer to cutting instructions on wrapper)
2-3 Tbsp. cold water

Figure 2-14. *Text showing auto spell checking is on*

I then spent time using my basic shapes tools and pen tools to create illustrations of various utensils and processes that relate to the instructions. If you don't know how something like a pastry blender looks, it's important to look at some images on the Internet as well as research how it is used. Refer to Figure 2-15.

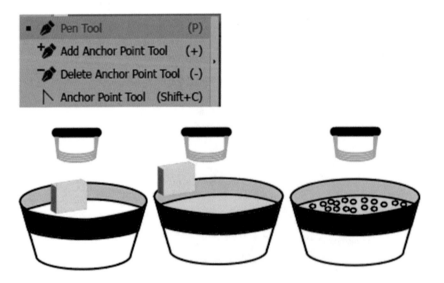

Figure 2-15. *Use the pen tools to draw various shapes. Illustration of a bowl in various stages of recipe progression with shortening that is cut with a pastry blender*

To indicate liquid water, I created a blue drop symbol by areas in the instructions where water was called for. Refer to Figure 2-16.

Figure 2-16. *Illustration of tablespoons of water poured into bowl, fork in bowl, and hands holding round ball of dough*

I also added a clock icon to indicate baking time and lines of steam to indicate that the pastry shell needs to cool. Refer to Figure 2-17.

Figure 2-17. *Illustration of a pie crust in a pan that needs to bake for 10 minutes and then cool with clock icon*

While most of the illustrations are two-dimensional, there are a few subtle 3D illustrations added as well. For example, creating the bricks of shortening was much easier to do using the 3D and Materials panel and setting the shape to Extrude with various depth lengths. For more details on this, you can refer to Volume 2. Refer to Figure 2-18.

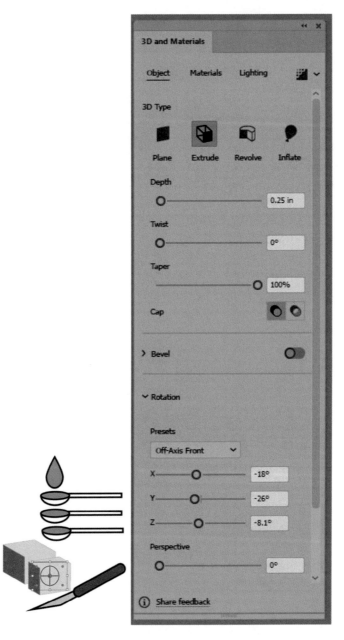

Figure 2-18. *Shortening with tablespoons, water droplet, and knife. Shortening brick was created with Object 3D Type Extrude settings found in the 3D and Materials panel*

I also used the 3D Extrusion setting on the rolling pin and handles, adjusting the Depth and Rotation and Perspective settings. Refer to Figure 2-19.

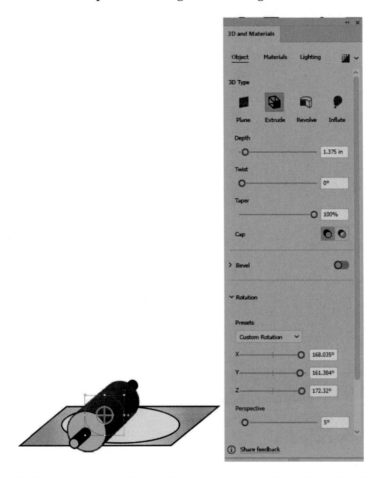

Figure 2-19. *Rolling pin with Object Extrude settings found in the 3D and Materials panel*

For a piece of pie at the end of the page on the right, I used the Revolve settings and lowered the revolve angle so that only a wedge of pie rather than the full ellipse was visible. Refer to Figure 2-20.

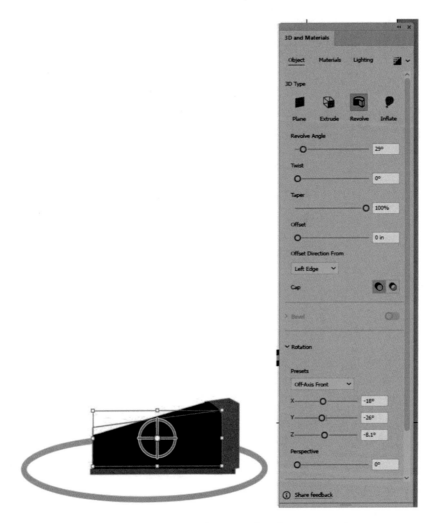

Figure 2-20. *3D illustration of a slice of pie with Object Revolve settings in the 3D and Materials panel*

As I created illustrations for related or sequential steps, I would Alt/Option+Drag out a copy of that item and then modify it either in shape or color so that the progression of the steps was a smoother transition. Refer to Figure 2-21.

Figure 2-21. *Illustration of a pie unbaked, backed, and a slice of pie with fork*

Some shapes I grouped together to make them easier to move or placed them on their own layer so that I would not move them if I selected the type or text by mistake. Refer to Figure 2-22.

Figure 2-22. *Layer panel with three visible layers*

Considerations

A few things to consider when building a project like this are

- How many illustrations will your client need?

- What sort of time do you need to complete the project they are giving you?

- Are these illustrations just for one article or a whole cookbook? If for a whole cookbook, then you need to consider what kind of layout application you need to use if the instructions fall on multiple pages. Learning how to lay out the text and various illustrations in InDesign which in that case would be a better solution.

- Again, you would also need to consider if the final layout will be for print or online. In this case, it was for print, so I made sure to add a guide layer, called Guides, so that I could place some guides at ¼ inch surrounding my print so that my printer did not cut off any important text or information.

Practice Your Design Skills

On your own, review my instructions page and consider the following:

- Could any of the steps be explained better with either more detailed text or a different illustration? For example, are more instructions needed on how to use the pastry blender or rolling out the dough?

- At the end of the instruction Step 7, a filling recipe was mentioned for the pie filling. After doing some research on your own, figure out some instructions for that and then sketch out how you would illustrate adding the filling to the pastry shell.

Example 3: 3D Wind Turbine Graph

While we saw in the pastry example some subtle uses of 3D again, when modifying a graph, as done in Volume 2, you can always add additional modifications to make the overall design appear more 3D like. Refer to the file WindTurbine_Graph.ai to review. Refer to Figure 2-23.

Figure 2-23. *Illustration of a graph with the columns representing wind turbines*

In this example, I use the 3D and Materials panel and my Selection Tool and Pen Tool to create some basic paths to create a 3D-like layout. This makes an interesting design on the topic of alternate energy and made the tops of the column graph resemble wind turbines as they disappear into the horizon. Refer to Figure 2-24.

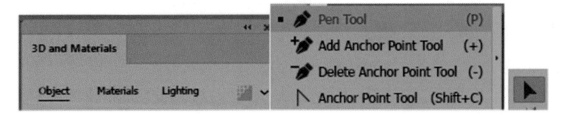

Figure 2-24. *3D and Materials panel, various pen tools, and the Selection Tool*

You may have to find an image of several wind turbines and study how they appear or trace over an image so that you can get the layout of the propellers at the correct size proportions. Remember, in your project, to keep your layers organized and then remove or turn off the visibility of the layers when you no longer need them. Refer to Figure 2-25.

Figure 2-25. *Layers panel with various layers and the trace layer's visibility turned off*

The 3D and Materials panel was used to create different object settings for the different parts of the turbine.

Each of the three blades used a setting of Inflate and a different rotation. Refer to Figures 2-26 and 2-27.

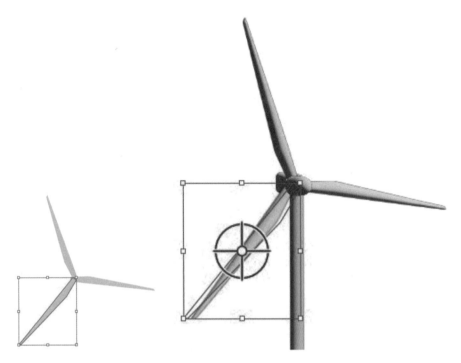

Figure 2-26. *Each blade path was set to Inflate using the 3D and Materials panel*

Figure 2-27. *3D and Materials panel with Object Tab and a setting of Inflate for the blades*

The rotor hub ellipse in the center and the rounded rectangle (gearbox/generator) in the back uses the setting of Extrude. However, the rotor hub had additional bevel settings applied to create the cone-like end. Select a shape with the Selection Tool to review exact settings for each item. Shapes have been placed behind and in front of each other using Object ➤ Arrange options. Refer to Figures 2-28 and 2-29.

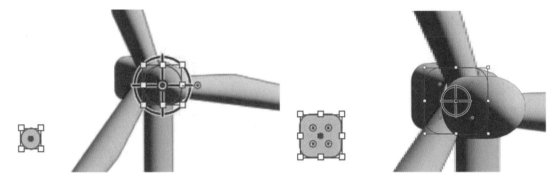

Figure 2-28. *The ellipse (rotor) and rounded rectangle (gearbox/generator) have a setting of Extrude in the 3D and Materials panel*

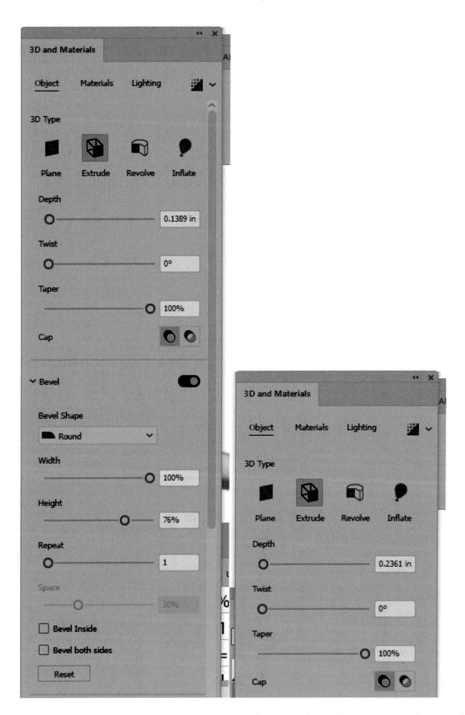

Figure 2-29. *3D and Materials Panel with Object Tab and a setting of Extrude for the circle and rounded rectangle*

You would then have to apply your own custom rotations for the x, y, and z axis. These can also be reviewed while that object is selected.

The tower is overlayed over the column on its own layer. It is a narrow rectangle with a setting of Revolve. Refer to Figure 2-30.

Figure 2-30. *3D and Materials panel with Object Tab and a setting of Revolve for the rectangular tower*

And the graph itself (behind the 3D illustration) and the lower text are using a setting of Object Plane with no extrusion. Refer to Figures 2-31 and 2-32.

Figure 2-31. *Illustration of wind turbine graph with the graph portion selected and set to a 3D Type of Plane*

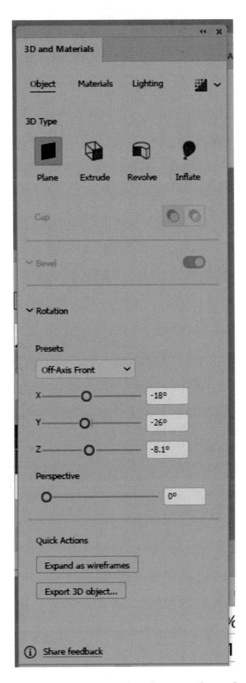

Figure 2-32. *3D and Materials panel with Object Tab and a setting of Plane for some type*

Graph text, as we saw in earlier examples in Volume 2, should have little or no extrusion as this can affect readability.

Note   Each of the heads of the wind turbines were scaled separately so that it gave the appearance they were getting smaller in the distance.

While each of the parts of the wind turbine has their own lighting, you must use the Lighting tab to modify the parts separately but keep the angles consistent so that the shading is constant with where you think the sun might be in the sky. In my case, it might have shined on them somewhere slightly behind me, so there would be no sun in the image. Refer to Figure 2-33.

Figure 2-33. *3D and Materials panel with Lighting tab and example of settings for parts of the wind turbine*

Creating the lower ground shadow is a bit tougher as you can easily create a shadow for the tower, but the upper parts of the wind turbine will not flow onto the same lower plane level as expected. Refer to Figure 2-34.

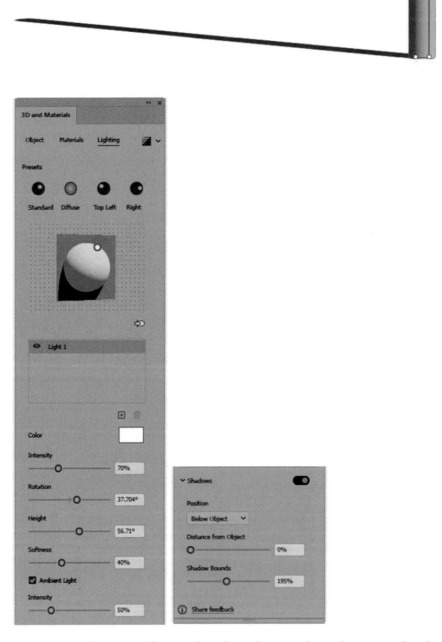

Figure 2-34. *3D and Materials panel with Lighting tab and settings for the tower*

In this case, you would need to create a 2D version of the propeller and rotor parts and group them together and make them black fill with no stroke. Refer to Figure 2-35.

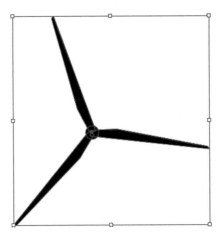

Figure 2-35. *Group paths to represent the top of the wind turbine*

To get a better perspective, I then experimented with the perspective plane of View ➤ Perspective Grid ➤ Two-Point Perspective ➤ 2P-Normal View and used the related tools which include the Plane switching widget, as seen in Volume 2. Refer to Figure 2-36.

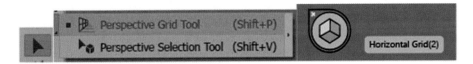

Figure 2-36. *Toolbars selection tools, Perspective Grid Tool, Perspective Selection Tool, and Plane switching widget*

I used the Horizontal Grid(2) plane and dragged copies of my grouped shapes onto it. To do that, I selected the path first, using the Selection Tool, and then used the Perspective Selection Tool to move, scale, and rotate on the grid until I was happy with the location. Refer to Figure 2-37 where I am just showing an example of one turbine.

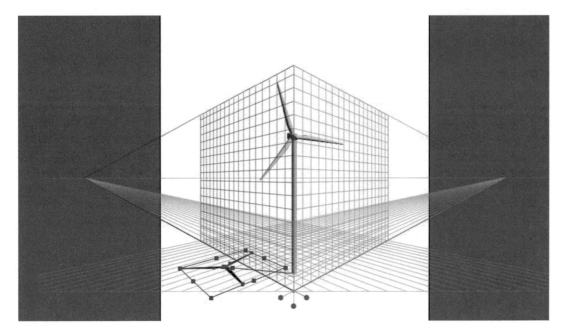

Figure 2-37. *Use the Perspective Grid Tool to lay out a shadow for the top of the turbine*

I followed this procedure for each of the wind turbines in my final example. Refer back the file wind_graph.ai.

Considerations

Designing a more specialized piece like this takes time and planning with your client, and both of you need a creative vision as to how you want the design to appear. In this case, because this is an infographic, you want to keep the area surrounding the graph relatively simplistic so that the design does not get lost in the background. In my case, I just added some grass, the sky, and a few symbol clouds from Illustrator's Nature set so that the concept of wind or movement is implied. Also, some type was added as part of legend off to the right-hand side to explain what the graph is about. Refer to Figure 2-38.

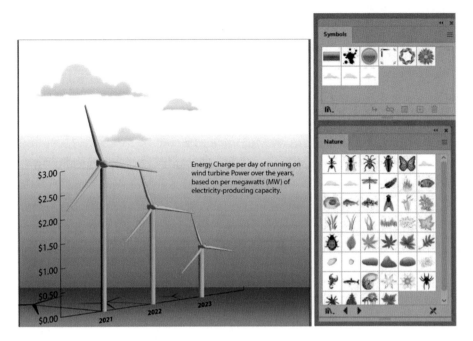

Figure 2-38. *Wind turbine graph and various symbols found in the Symbols panel and Nature Library*

This layout leaves space for surrounding text, which should more be added later in an application like InDesign, as mentioned in Chapter 3.

Note that for this example, you may need to flatten the final artwork in Photoshop and save in a (.tif) format to ensure that the graphic renders correctly if used in InDesign as part of a page layout. I will mention how to do that in Chapter 3 in regard to the 3D coffee graph that was created in Volume 2.

Practice Your Design Skills

On your own, try designing a graph that has some 3D effects, or think of a creative way that a graph could represent some everyday objects but still represent a graph. Remember, of all the graphing tools, column, bar, and pie are usually the best to experiment with. Try to find a balance between the design and the data so that the information you want to convey is not lost to the audience but is engaging as well as easy to read.

Example 4: Safe Driver Electric Car Poster

As the infographic becomes more complex and there is more text and objects, you may want to set your artboard to a larger page size such as Legal or 11 × 17 inches landscape. If the folded size of a magazine is 8½ × 11 inches, then this page size could be easily added to the magazine at its center or as an insert on the side.

In this case, for printing reasons as with the earlier recipe example, I would make sure to again leave a ¼ inch of space around the four sides of poster should trimming later be required. I would set this up with my rulers and guides on a layer ahead of time and also add guides to the center at 8½ inches and at ¼ inch on each side so that I could see where the poster might fold if it were inside a magazine. While guides never print, as mentioned, I would put them on their own locked layer so that I can turn the visibility on and off as I work. Refer to Figure 2-39.

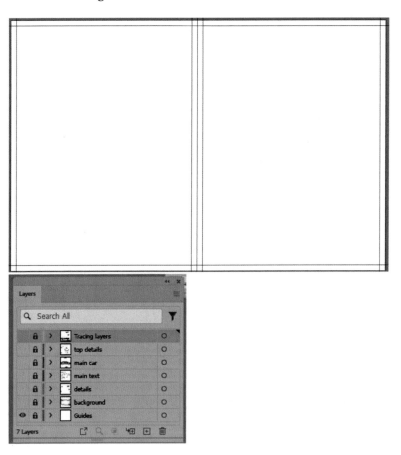

Figure 2-39. *Guides on artboard and Layers panel with various layers visibility turned off and the guides layer visible*

The layout of guides will vary based on page size and print recommendations by the publishing or print house.

In this case, I put together some safety tips and car care tips for drivers of electric vehicles (EV). Refer to the file safe_driver.ai. Refer to Figure 2-40.

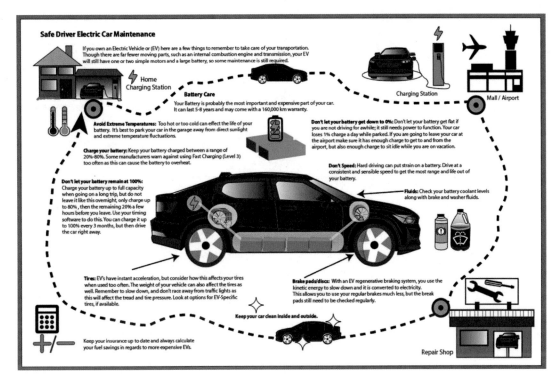

Figure 2-40. *Poster layout of Safe Driver Electric Car Maintenance*

If you or a client have an electric vehicle, you may want to take a few pictures of it ahead of time. You can then place the images in Illustrator for drawing and tracing purposes, on their own tracing layer above or below the other layers, and then lock this layer. Then use the pen tools, selection tools, and Control panel, as in other projects, to make modifications to the design over the images. On your paths, later select strokes and colors so that they fit your layout. Refer to Figure 2-41.

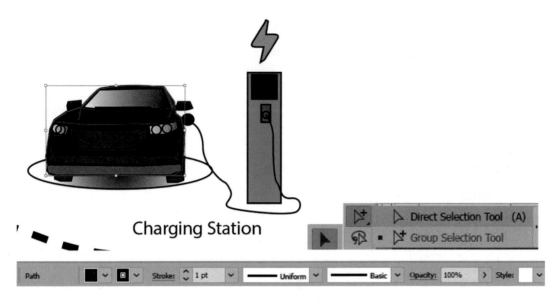

Figure 2-41. *Illustration of the electric car at charging station with part of the object's path selected, the selection tools and the selected fill and stroke appearing in the Control panel*

In the current example, the tips and illustrations in this layout are displayed in such a way that this could be a poster viewed in an office or classroom setting. There is a lot of text and detail in this example, but ultimately it tells one story on how to care for the parts of your electric vehicle.

We can see the car at home in the garage, plugged into the charging station, and then as it journeys on the road or dashed line to its next destination, the airport or mall, where there is a charging station, to keep the battery at optimum levels. Then the car travels to the repair shop for a tune-up and finally returns home. Refer to Figure 2-42.

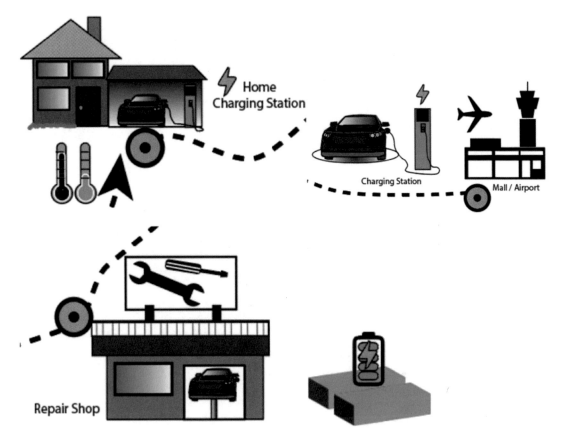

Figure 2-42. *Illustrations of the electric vehicle in various locations and then 3D batteries*

In the center of the infographic page are most of the tips in regard to the battery care tips, but also some other things to consider, like checking your fluids as well as tires and brake pads/discs. Using gradients can also give the appearance of shadows as well and can be modified using the Gradient panel; they are stored in the Swatches panel and later accessed using the Control or Properties panel. Refer to Figure 2-43.

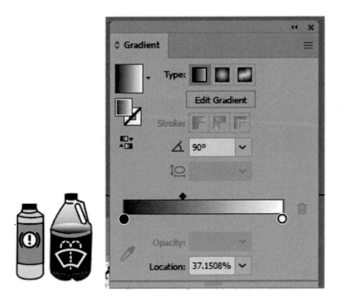

Figure 2-43. *Illustrations of fluids for the car and the Gradient panel*

There is also a reminder to keep your car clean and the insurance up to date as well, but the immediate reminders surround the larger car. Refer to Figure 2-40 and Figure 2-44.

Figure 2-44. *Illustration of calculation icons and a clean car driving on a dashed line*

The vehicle in the center of the page in this case is enlarged and shows, in more detail, important parts which are identified with arrows pointing at them and supplemental text. Refer to Figures 2-40 and 2-45.

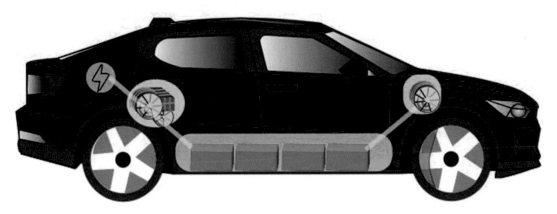

Figure 2-45. *Electric vehicle illustration looking inside and the motor and batteries*

As well there are semitransparent cutaways using the Transparency panel to change the paths opacity. This is done so that we can understand where the plug is inserted for charging and how charging keeps the batteries active, as well as where some of the main motors are located in certain models. Refer to Figure 2-46.

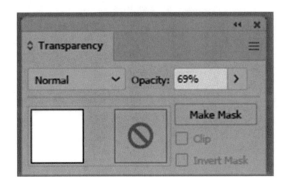

Figure 2-46. *Transparency panel with a new Opacity setting*

These motors and batteries, like other examples, have a 3D effect using the 3D and Materials panel applied to them of Extrude but are then overlayed with some lines so that the design blends in with the semi-2D/3D appearance of the other illustrations. In this case, adding a stroke to the main path gave better shadows. Refer to Figures 2-47 and 2-48.

Figure 2-47. *Control panel setting for the selected ellipse on the motor illustration*

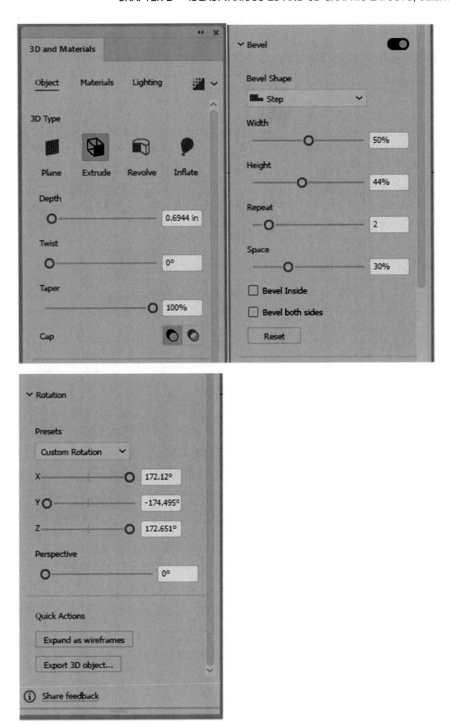

Figure 2-48. *3D and Materials panel with settings in the Lighting Object Tab for Extrude*

Lighting again had to have a custom adjustment for each part. Refer to Figure 2-49.

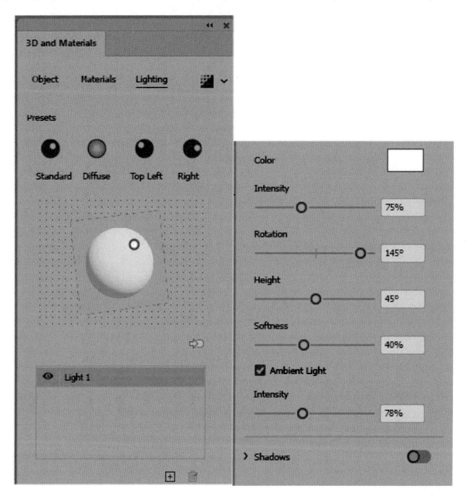

Figure 2-49. *3D and Materials panel with settings in the Lighting tab*

A few icons and simplified shapes are also placed here and there to indicate temperature, a plane at an airport, tools at a repair shop, and a calculator to consider costs. Refer to Figure 2-50.

Figure 2-50. *Illustrations representing temperature and calculations*

In this case, because the poster is for the public, we are not trying to overwhelm them with too much technical design, but just enough to give the highlights of EV maintenance.

Considerations

If you are designing a similar poster or a process for your client, consider the following:

- What are the main tips or steps that you need to include?

- If it will be a large format poster, like 11 × 17 inches, you may be able to include more text, but what if it had to be 8½ × 11, what would you include or remove so that it fits the layout?

- What if the poster were instead for a repair or mechanic's shop where workers were receiving on-the-job training? Which areas of the poster might require more or different details?

Practice Your Design Skills

Alternatively, design a poster on a process or topic that interests you. Remember to research the topic first, and then, as with the recipe example, type out the steps and keep them on their own layer or layers so that as you add the illustrations, they don't move around. Then, if required, and you have photos, trace over your images (which are on their own separate locked layer) with your basic shapes or pen tools, using your Selection Tool and Object ➤ Arrange options to arrange your sublayers. Then color each fill and stroke as required using the Layers, Swatches, and Control panels.

Designing and laying out your poster may take several days as it takes time to arrange your overall concept. Make sure, if this is for a client, to send them updates of your design as a PDF (see Chapter 3 for more details). Or create a screen capture and print it out as you develop the design and review your layout changes and adjustments with them. As the layout progresses, you will see gaps or areas you missed and then decide if you need to add more or take away portions to make the layout balanced.

As each design you create is unique, there is no easy way of giving instructions on how complex infographic should be. However, with Illustrator, you have an arsenal of tools ready anytime. With time, practice, and increasing skill, you can make you and your client's concept and ideas a reality.

Reviewing Your Completed Infographic with Your Client

After you have completed your infographic design, make sure to review the design with your client before the final sign-off. Any last-minute changes should be minor at this stage, such as spell-checking or moving an item within the infographic so that it fits within the allotted area on the printed page or web page.

Making Final Changes and Adjustments

However, as mentioned earlier, as the infographic is about to be published, there may be a sudden last-minute new details added, as we can see in institutions where the data is continuously changing, such as in science, finance, banking, real estate, and politics. If the infographic, as we have seen, is a simple chart or graph design, data changes may be very minor and easy to make in the graph data window table cells, and the change can instantly be reflected in the graph upon committing the change as seen in Volume 2. Refer to Figure 2-51.

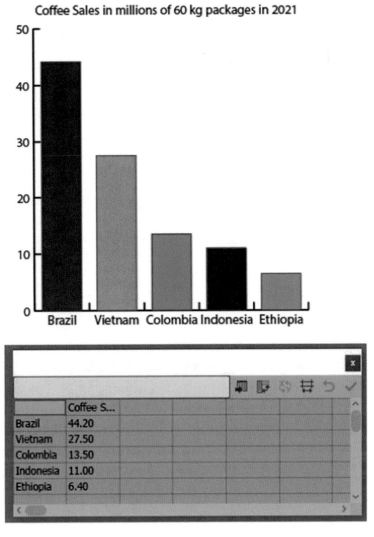

Figure 2-51. *Column graph and graph data window table cells*

However, when it comes to illustration or complex 3D shapes or additions to animation or video, the alternation may take longer. These are all things to consider with the client. Questions to ask:

- Are the new details necessary on short notice?

- Is it possible to add them on a short deadline, or can they be added to the next publication?

- Does the change fit with your approved budget?

- Will the change affect what the viewer needs to know currently?

Prior research of a topic will certainly give you clues as to whether or not this topic changes from year to year or day to day. Frequently changing data will likely need to be simplified in an easy-to-update infographic, but as you have seen in this chapter's examples, this should not prevent you from being creative within the time frame.

Once you have made your final changes, you will want to save the file in the format the client or publisher requires. We saw this in Chapter 1 for SVG files, but we looked at other formats such as PDF in Chapter 3.

As with any files, always save a backup of your work in an (.ai) format and then consider adding the designs to your personal printed and online portfolio.

Learning from Feedback

After the infographic is published, if you know the website it is published on, or that your client will be receiving comments/feedback from the public or other colleagues, you should certainly ask your client to let you know what others thought of the design, especially if it may be published again with new data in the future. In a lot of cases, it is likely you won't hear a lot about the infographic unless someone notices an inaccuracy or someone is a fan of what you have designed. Your fan base might include the public, fellow students, coworkers, or others in education. Yes, in a way, you have now become an influencer. Regardless, any feedback, positive or negative, can be helpful in knowing how to improve and produce an even better infographic the next time.

New Panels to Explore on Your Own

While not mentioned in this book, Adobe Illustrator CC 2024 has added some new panels and features that may extend how you plan to use your infographic and logos. On your own, make sure to check them out. In Volume 1, you looked at Generative Recolor and Retype (Beta). However, another new feature you may want to try is Text to Vector Graphic (Beta) powered by Adobe Firefly. You can access this panel either from the Window menu or directly from the Properties panel. When you don't require it, you can just collapse the toggle in the Properties panel which you will see in the upper area. This feature is very similar to Generative Recolor in the sense that you can use text prompts, but this time they can be used to generate a subject, scene, icon, or even a pattern from a selected rectangular path rather than build the item yourself from scratch. In the case of patterns, they can be reedited using the Pattern Options panel as directed in Volume 2. Our focus in these volumes was to explore drawing your own creations using your own artistic abilities, but you can learn more about this panel from the following links as well as its current user guidelines due to the fact that it is currently in beta.

`https://helpx.adobe.com/illustrator/using/text-to-vector-graphic.html`

`www.adobe.com/legal/licenses-terms/adobe-gen-ai-user-guidelines.html`

The other new panel that you can access from the Window menu that you may want to explore after you have created your mock-ups as mentioned in Volume 1 is the new Mockup (Beta) panel. This could be a useful option rather than entering Photoshop to paste your layout of a logo or text on photos of packaging and promotional items. Instead, you can use this panel to finalize your layout. To access this area currently requires a separate install. Also, because it is beta this feature is subject to change. You can learn more about it at the following link:

`https://helpx.adobe.com/illustrator/using/create-art-mockups.html`

Summary

In this chapter, we reviewed various examples of infographic ideas and project possibilities. Later you considered how to work with your client on the final review of your project and the importance of learning from feedback.

In the next chapter, we will be looking at what are the next steps for exporting your infographic and using it in other Adobe applications that are part of the Creative Cloud workflow.

Next Steps with Infographics Using Adobe Creative Cloud

In this chapter, we will be looking at how to save and export your infographic file in various formats and considering what other Adobe applications in the Creative Cloud you could use to continue the layout of your infographic.

As a graphic designer, Illustrator does not have to be the last stop as you create your infographic. In this chapter, we will look at what are the final steps in Illustrator for saving your file and then what other applications can be used to further enhance your infographic.

Note This chapter does contain examples of projects that can be found in the Volume 3 Chapter 3 folder.

Formats to Save Your Infographic

Let's review and look at a few more formats for saving your infographics using Illustrator.

Final File Formats (.ai, .eps, .pdf)

Often, for printing, if you need to submit your final files to clients or on their behalf for a print or online publication, you should use the following formats. However, always consult with your printing company or client first that they can open these formats, and

© Jennifer Harder 2023
J. Harder, *Creating Infographics with Adobe Illustrator: Volume 3*,
https://doi.org/10.1007/979-8-8688-0038-2_3

if there are any other settings for these formats, you need to account for such as color profile setting, page layout, or alternate file format choices. For print situations, let's look at these three formats when you choose File ➤ Save or File ➤ Save As and save on your computer. Refer to Figure 3-1.

Figure 3-1. *Save on your computer button*

- (.ai) Adobe Illustrator
- (.eps) Illustrator EPS
- (.pdf) Adobe PDF

Adobe Illustrator (.ai)

To review, the (.ai) file, as mentioned in this book and the previous volumes, is best for working with all the functions of Adobe Illustrator when designing your file. If your client or print company has the same version of Adobe Illustrator, they should be able to successfully open your file. However, if they have an older version of the application such as pre-2020, they may not be able to open the (.ai) file, or you may have to choose a downsaved version. If that is the case, be aware that new features that have been applied to the design may be lost. This could include gradients or the appearance of certain effects or transparency.

As mentioned in Volume 1, when I save a new file in this format, generally for print, I start with the color mode of CMYK. However, if you have been asked to save as RGB or have already been working in RGB and need to switch to CMYK for a copy of the file afterward, remember to use File ➤ Document Color Mode. Refer to Figure 3-2.

Document Setup...	Alt+Ctrl+P		
Document Color Mode	>	✓	CMYK Color
File Info...	Alt+Shift+Ctrl+I		RGB Color

Figure 3-2. *File Document Color Mode options CMYK and RGB*

Note   Unless instructed otherwise, leave your Edit ➤ Color settings and Edit ➤ Assign Profile settings as is.

To review, after you have clicked Save to save your file in a selected location on your computer, your Illustrator Options panel dialog box will allow you to choose a compatible version. Use the list if you need to downsave for older applications, but by default, you should leave the setting at Illustrator 2020. Refer to Figures 3-3 and 3-4.

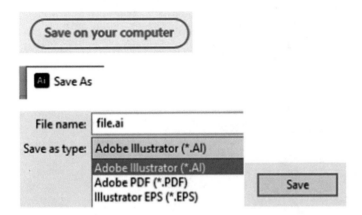

Figure 3-3. *Save on your computer button the Save As dialog box with a Save as type of Adobe Illustrator (*.AI)*

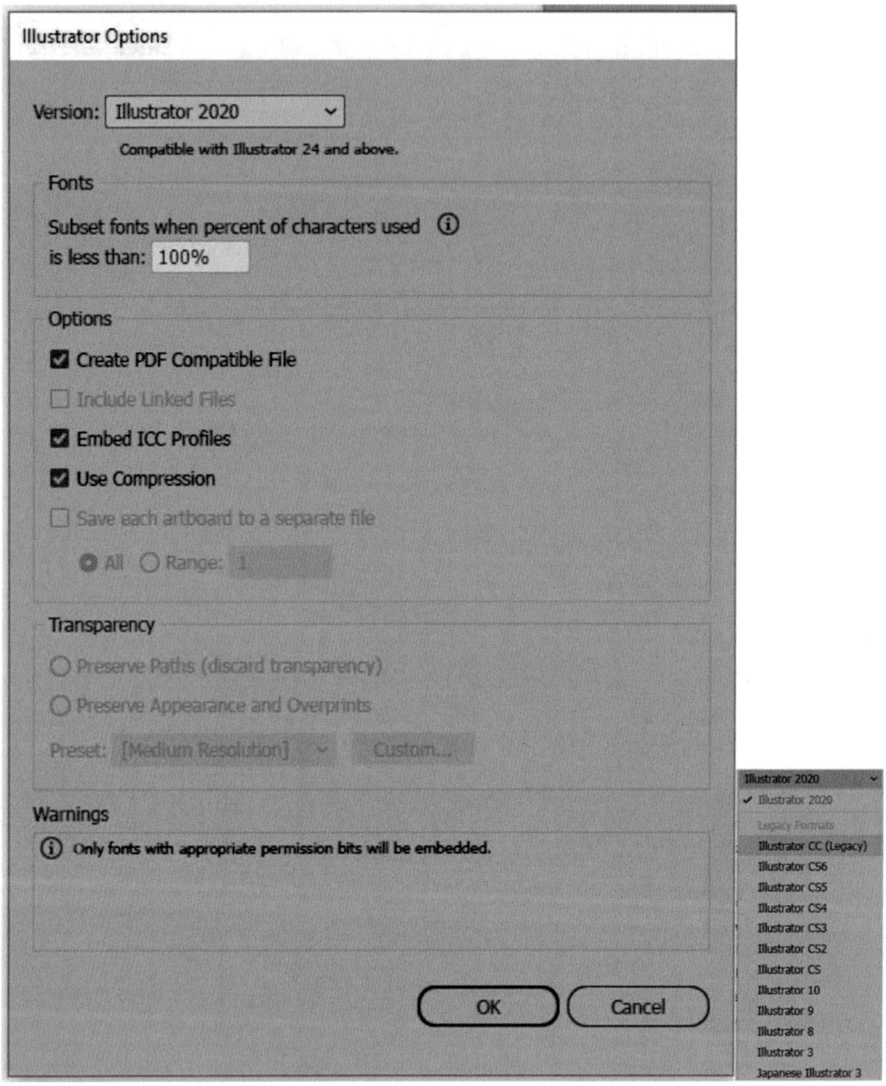

Figure 3-4. *Settings in the Illustrator Options dialog box*

Leave the Fonts setting for Subset fonts when percent of characters used is less than 100%.

Keep the Options at the default of Create PDF Compatible File so that you can use the file with other Adobe applications.

Include Linked files if Preset is optional; you can leave this unchecked if you do not have any linked images to include or want to embed, which will increase your file's size. Otherwise, you will want to make sure those images are in the same folder as the (.ai) file when you send the final document to be printed.

The Embed ICC Profiles for color management check box should be enabled.

Use Compression check box should be enabled to compress PDF data; however, unchecking may speed up the saving time if the file saves very slowly.

Save each artboard as a separate file can be left unchecked; unless you have multiple artboards, then you can set all or a range. If there is only one artboard, then this area is disabled.

For Transparency, you can determine what happens to transparent objects when you choose a version of Illustrator format earlier than 9.0 such as 8 or 3. In that case, options would be available such as either Preserve Paths (discard transparency) or Preserve Appearance and Overprints; by default, the preset remains at medium resolution, but if available, you can set custom settings. If there are items with transparency and you are using Version Illustrator 2020, they will remain at the default options, and this area will be disabled as Transparency is not a concern for newer Illustrator files.

Based on version settings, review any warnings in this example for 2020, "Only the fonts with appropriate permission bits will be embedded." As mentioned, in Volume 1, to ensure that a specific font remains in a document for print in your copy, prior to saving, you may have to use Type ➤ Create Outlines. You would then click OK to complete saving the file.

Illustrator EPS (.eps)

The (.eps) is another file format option that you can use with your print company or client if they cannot open the (.ai) format. EPS files can also be opened in some other applications as well. However, be aware that while most design elements of an EPS will display identically to (.ai), you should still always keep an (ai) backup as well. After you have selected a Location and clicked Save, here are the settings that appear in the EPS Options dialog box. Refer to Figures 3-5 and 3-6.

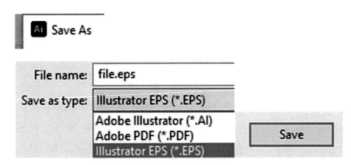

Figure 3-5. *Save As dialog box with a Save as type of Illustrator EPS (*.EPS)*

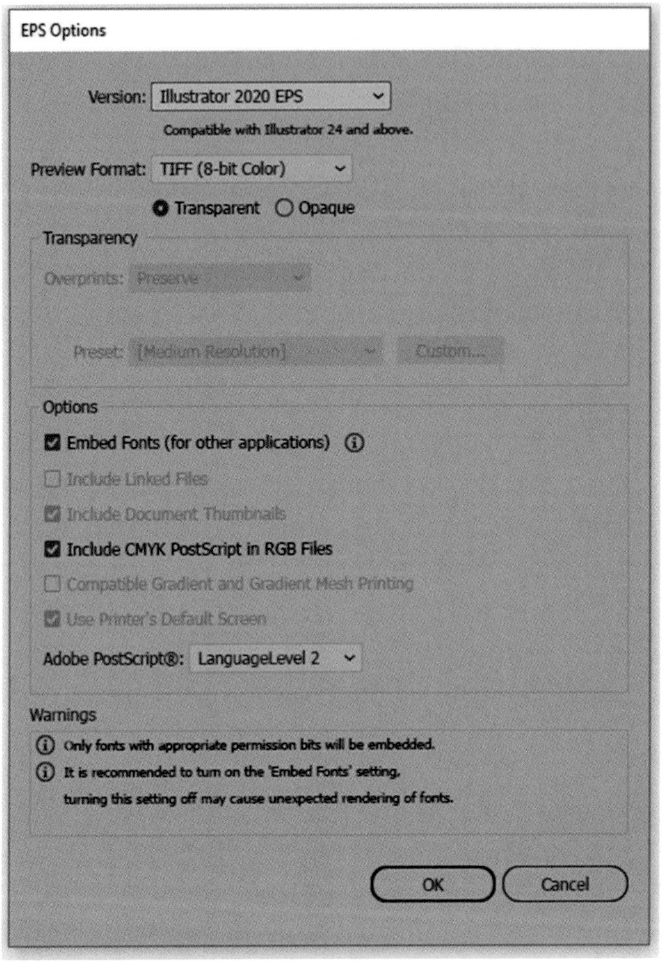

Figure 3-6. *Settings in the EPS Options dialog box*

Version: As with the AI file, you can downsave your version for older applications by selecting an option from the list. This may alter some of the options you see in the dialog box. However, it is best to keep the settings at the default of Illustrator 2020 EPS.

The preview format by default is set to TIFF (8-bit color), which allows for Transparent and Opaque options. However, other options include TIFF (Black and White) and None. In this case, for best results, I would leave the settings at TIFF (8-bit color) and the radio button at Transparent especially if you place and link the file in an application like InDesign. Having transparency around the shapes is best rather than a white background area (opaque) that might block other items behind the infographic.

Transparency settings, if available, can be set for Overprints to Preserve; the default for the Preset for Transparency is [Medium Resolution], but [High Resolution], [Low Resolution], and [For Complex Art] options are available as well; you can set custom settings as well for dealing with Raster/Vector Balance and other advanced settings involving line art, text, and gradients. Refer to Figure 3-7.

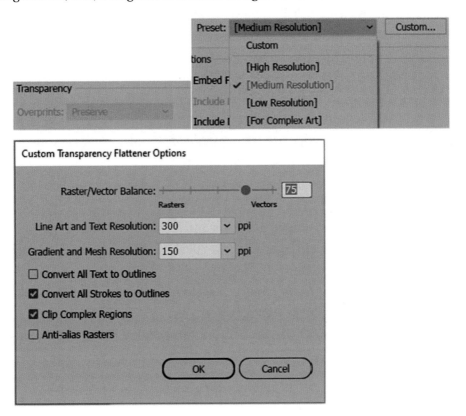

Figure 3-7. *Transparency settings in the EPS Options dialog box and the Custom Transparency Flattener Options dialog box*

Options found in the EPS Options dialog box include

Embed Fonts (for other applications): This is enabled, and you can review the following informational warning in the following for this setting. In this case, only fonts with appropriate permission bits will be embedded, and it is recommended to turn on the "Embed Fonts" settings because turning this setting off may cause unexpected rendering of fonts. If a computer that opens the file in Illustrator does not have that font installed, it may be faux or substituted. Refer to Figure 3-6.

Include Linked files: If there are linked files, this option will be available, otherwise, the option is disabled. Files will be embedded if enabled. Refer to Figure 3-6.

Include Document Thumbnails is checked by default: This creates a type of preview of the image when viewed upon opening or placing the image. Refer to Figure 3-6.

Include CMYK PostScript in RGB Files is checked by default, so both kinds of color information are preserved. This allows RGB color documents to be printed from applications that do not support the RGB Color Mode output. Refer to Figure 3-6.

Compatible Gradient and Gradient Mesh Printing: If gradients or gradient meshes have been used in the artwork, this option will be available to check. According to Adobe, this option enables older printers and PostScript devices to print gradients and gradient meshes by converting gradient objects to JPEG format. However, selecting this option can slow print on newer printers that don't have problems with gradients; by default, this setting is unchecked. Refer to Figure 3-6.

Use Printer's Default Screen is checked by default. Refer to Figure 3-6.

Currently, the Adobe PostScript Language is set to LanguageLevel 2 by default, and that is fine for most vector and bitmap color images, but it can be set to LanguageLevel 3 if required and may be useful to do so if you are dealing with objects that contain gradients or a gradient mesh. Refer to Figure 3-6.

For more details on this option setting, as well as for AI Settings and SVG mentioned in Chapter 1, you can refer to the following page:

`https://helpx.adobe.com/illustrator/using/saving-artwork.html`

Illustrator PDF (.pdf)

Use the (.pdf) Portable Document Format in situations where you have a completed or final document that you want to print. Likewise, you can use it as part of your online portfolio for your website. PDFs can be reopened in Illustrator or Photoshop; however, these files are often compressed, and you may discover some quality or information loss if you try to edit the file. Make sure to make a (.ai) copy of the artwork if you plan to do some future editing. Refer to Figure 3-8.

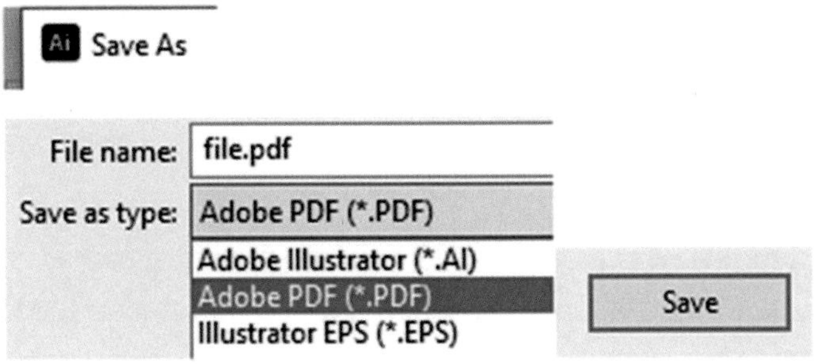

Figure 3-8. *Save As dialog box with a Save as type of Adobe PDF (*.PDF)*

The Save PDF dialog box has many additional settings and tabs. Refer to Figure 3-9.

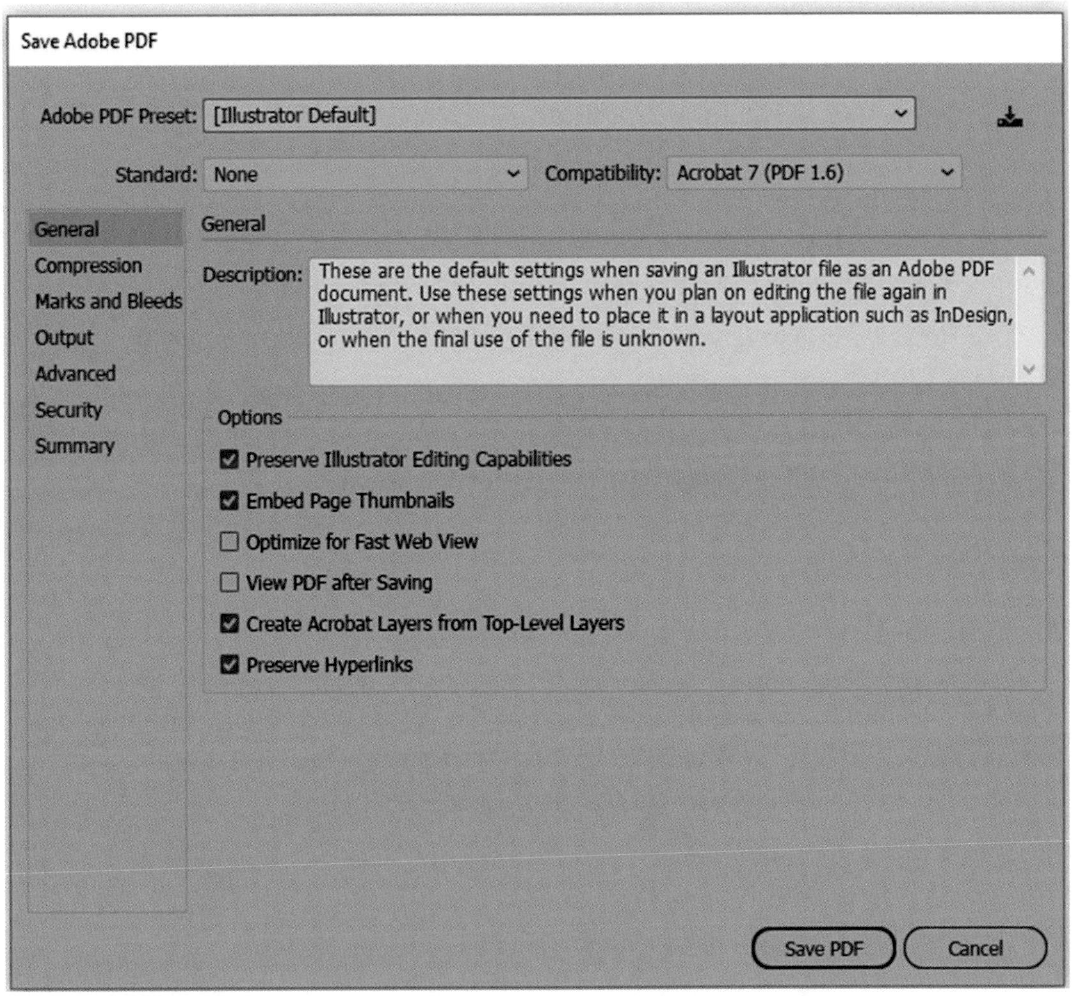

Figure 3-9. *Save Adobe PDF dialog box General tab*

While I will not go into a lot of detail here, I will just point out the main tabs and settings.

General Tab

First, you will need to review the General tab and the preceding area (refer to Figure 3-9), which displays the Adobe PDF Preset, Standard is set to none, and the Compatibility is set to Acrobat 7 (PDF 1.6); click the downward arrow icon on the upper right if you need to save any preset settings. In the General area, you will want to review the description to see whether the current settings are OK; if you plan to open your file in Illustrator again, plan to place a linked file in InDesign, or when the final use of the file is unknown. I generally keep the options at the default of

- **Preserve Illustrator Editing Capabilities**: Check box enabled.

- **Embed Page Thumbnails**: Check box enabled.

- **Optimize for Fast Web View**: Check box disabled.

- **View PDF after Saving**: Check box disabled, unless you want it to open automatically in Acrobat Pro, then check this option.

- **Create Acrobat Layers from Top-Level Layers**: Check box enabled.

- **Preserve Hyperlinks**: Check box enabled; this is good if the text does contain links to websites that you want to preserve for a PDF that will be online, but not necessarily for a print document.

Compression Tab

This area is more for if your files have bitmap images that will be embedded, which are either color, grayscale, or monochrome. By default, these options will be set to "Do not Downsample" and Compression: Zip. However, you can set other Compression options that affect image quality; by default, it is set to 8-bit. Refer to the link at the end of this section if you need more details. Refer to Figure 3-10.

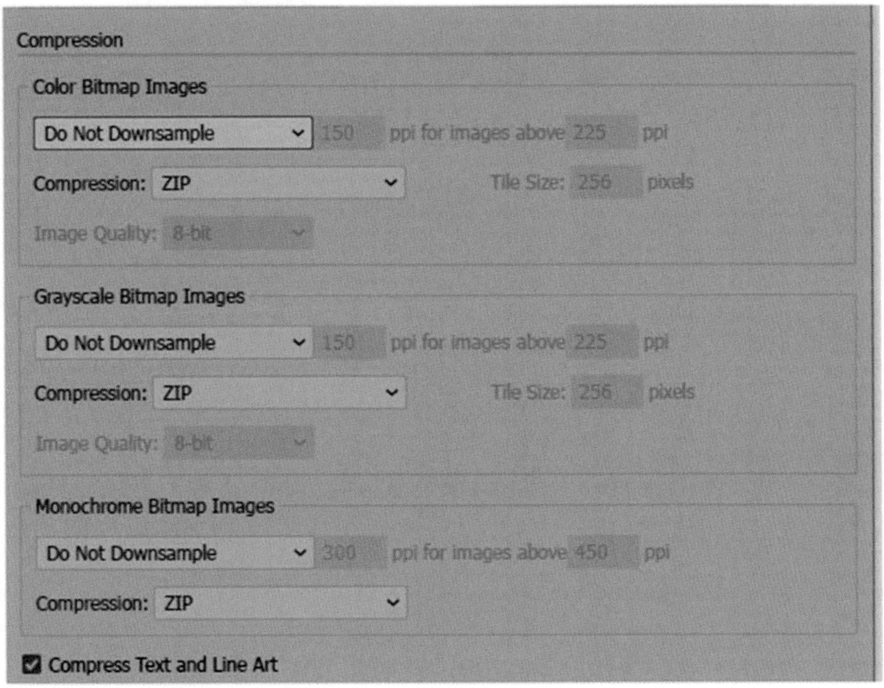

Figure 3-10. *Save Adobe PDF dialog box Compression tab*

By default, Compress Text and Line Art check box is enabled.

Marks and Bleeds Tab

If you are not familiar with what printer marks are, then leave this setting at the default. In this case, the following should be unchecked: All Printer's Marks, Trim Marks, Registration Marks, Color Bars, and Page Information. Leave Printer Mark Type at Roman, and leave the Trim Mark Weight at 0.25pt and Offset at 6pt. Refer to Figure 3-11.

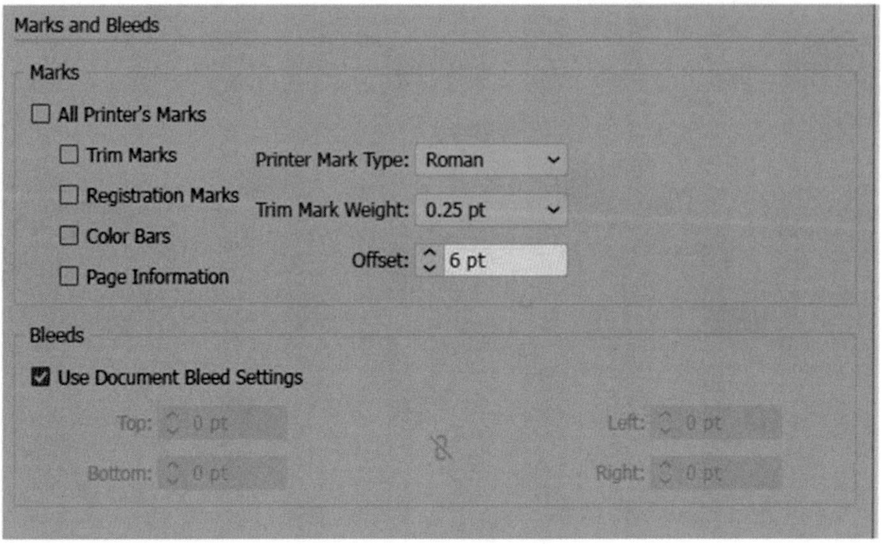

Figure 3-11. Save Adobe PDF dialog box Marks and Bleeds tab

Leave the Bleeds at Use Document Bleed Settings enabled. In this case, I left it at 0pt for Top, Bottom, Left, and Right as this was not part of the discussion of this book. If the print company you are working with mentions that you need to add Marks or Bleeds, consult with them on the steps for doing this, or they may just request that you send the (.ai) or (.eps) file and then may add these themselves.

Output Tab

This tab refers to the Color output and the settings for the PDF/X Type for graphics. In this case, you can leave these at the default of

- **Color Conversion**: No Conversion.

- **Destination**: N/A.

- **Profile Inclusion Policy "Don't Include Profiles."**

- **PDF/X**: This area will, in this case, remain disabled, but this is a more advanced area that affects color profiles and management, and you can refer to the details on this topic in the link provided in this section.

Hover over an item, and the Description area will give you a hint as to what the setting means. Refer to Figure 3-12.

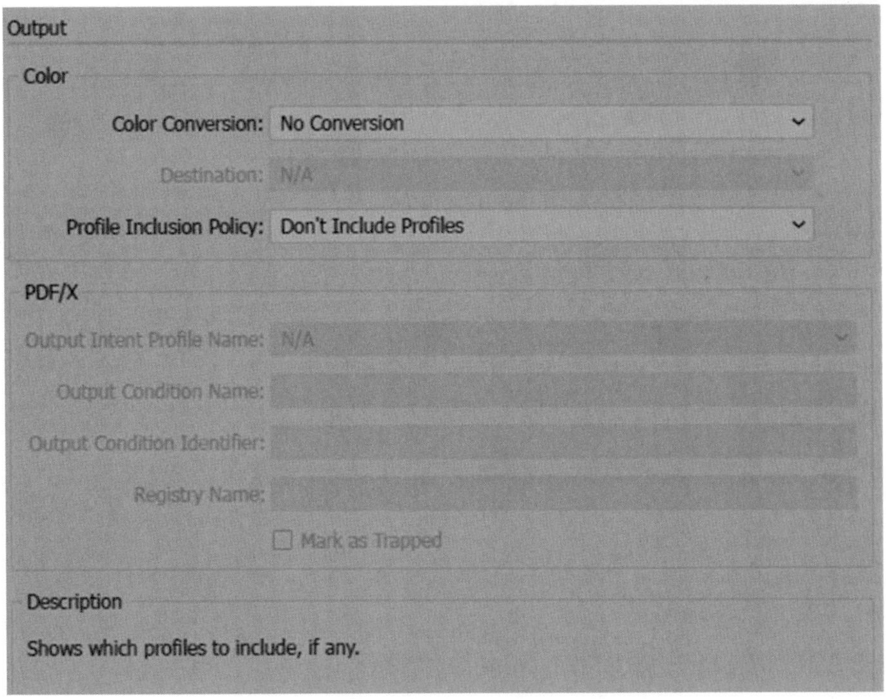

Figure 3-12. *Save Adobe PDF dialog box Output tab*

In this book, we will not be focused on these settings but speak to your printing company if they need you to alter these settings from the default. Refer to Figure 3-12.

Advanced Tab

The Advanced tab allows you to adjust the setting for Fonts "Subset fonts when percent of characters used is less than 100%." All fonts with appropriate embedding bits will be embedded. For older PDF version 1.3. Only, you can set the Overprint and Transparency Flattener Options. In this case, this area is disabled since you are using Acrobat 7 (PDF 1.6) and it is left at the default Overprints: Preserve and Preset [Medium Resolution]. Leave these settings at their default. Refer to Figure 3-13.

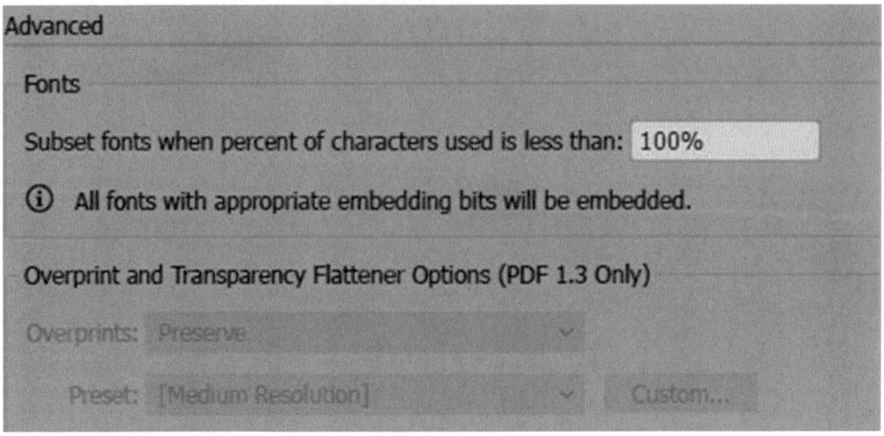

Figure 3-13. *Save Adobe PDF dialog box Advanced tab*

Security Tab

Only use the Security area when you want to password protect your PDF such as for your online portfolio, but not when you want your print company to print the file. If for your online portfolio, you can choose to set the password upon opening the document to be prompted, or if open and someone else wants to edit the PDF document, they must first enter the password. Otherwise, they will not be able to make edits to your file without permission. Refer to Figure 3-14.

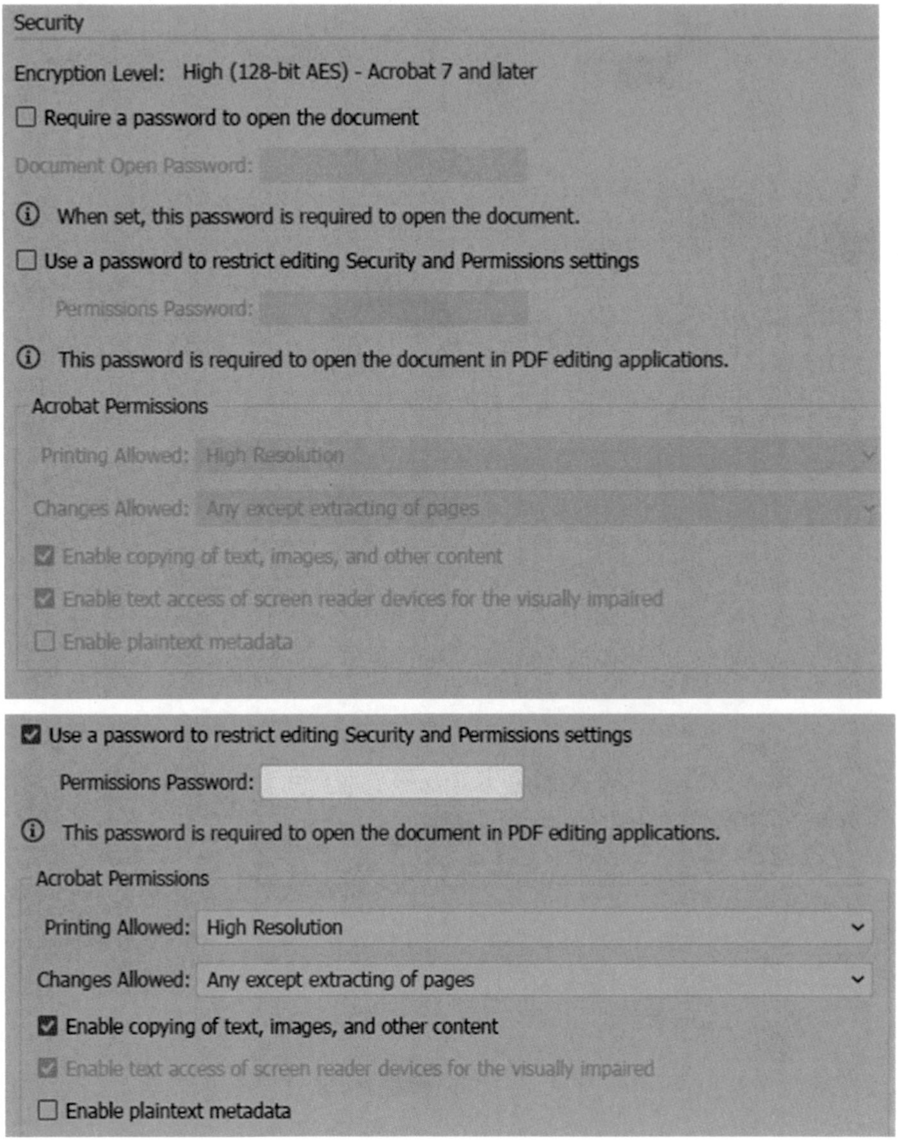

Figure 3-14. *Save Adobe PDF dialog box Security tab*

Security settings can include such things as various Acrobat Permissions:

- **Printing Allowed**: As certain settings are allowed (none, high, or low resolution). Refer to Figure 3-15.

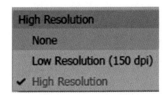

Figure 3-15. *Save Adobe PDF dialog box Security tab, Printing Allowed settings*

- **Changes Allowed**: To the document (none, any except extracting of pages, inserting, rotating, and deleting pages, commenting, and filling in form fields). Refer to Figure 3-16.

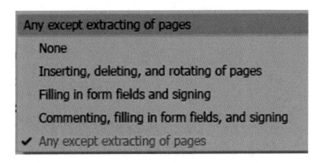

Figure 3-16. *Save Adobe PDF dialog box Security tab, Changes Allowed settings*

- Enable whether you can copy text, images, and other content out of the PDF.

- Enable text access for screen reader devices for the visually impaired. This is set by default to enabled.

- Enable plaintext metadata; by default, it is unchecked. Refer to Figure 3-14.

Note   Some of these settings may only relate to Acrobat Pro and not items created in Illustrator such as filling in form fields and signing, so by default, I leave these Security settings disabled for print work. If you do add a password you may be altered to enter it one more time when you click the Save PDF button.

Summary Tab

This area summarizes any options you may have chosen as well as any warnings that may appear. You can also save your summary, if required, in this case, to save the PDF, you would click the Save PDF button or Cancel to not save your settings and exit. Refer to Figure 3-17.

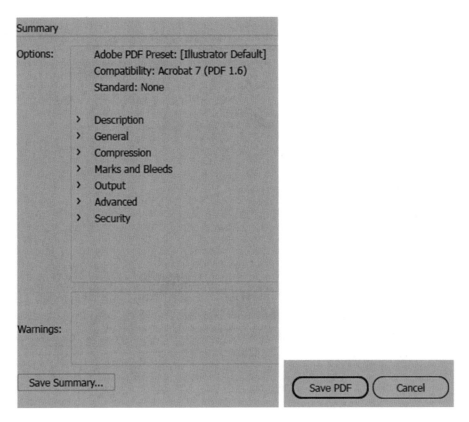

Figure 3-17. *Save Adobe PDF dialog box Summary tab*

For full details on saving a PDF file, you can refer to the following pages:

https://helpx.adobe.com/illustrator/using/creating-pdf-files.html

https://helpx.adobe.com/illustrator/using/pdf-options.html

While you can create a PDF of the whole artboard using File ➤ Save As or Save a Copy for small assets, it would be faster to use the Asset Export panel, which we will review next.

Asset Export Panel

As mentioned in Volume 2 and Chapter 1 of this volume, the Asset Export panel can be used to save 3D files and SVG files. However, you can save other formats which include PDF, but also the traditional raster/pixelated files that you use on a website, such as PNG and JPEG that come in various quality settings that are noted by the number by the file format name, for example, JPG 20 would be lower quality than JPG 100. Refer to Figure 3-18.

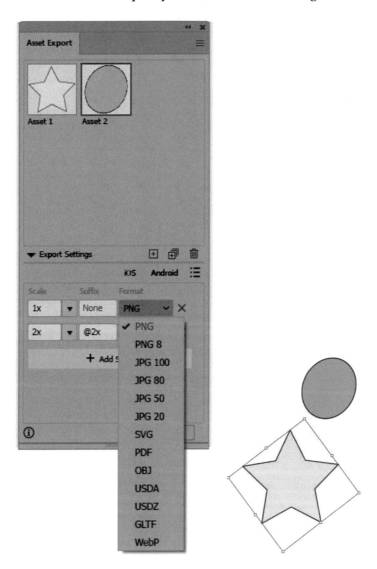

Figure 3-18. *Asset Export Panel with paths and shapes with effects in the panel and on the Artboard, with one on the Artboard selected*

Assets that are selected on the Artboard and in the Assets Export panel can be easily updated in the Assets panel before you choose to export the final file in any of the available scale and format options. Refer to Figure 3-19.

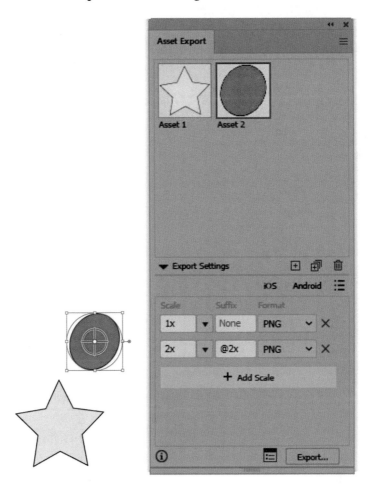

Figure 3-19. *Asset Export Panel with paths and shapes with effects in the panel and on the Artboard selected and updated in the panel*

However, I will point out a new web format that has recently been introduced into Photoshop and Illustrator, which is the WebP file. With any of the earlier mentioned settings, if you want to review the options of a specific format, you need to click the Format Settings in the Options menu. Refer to Figure 3-20.

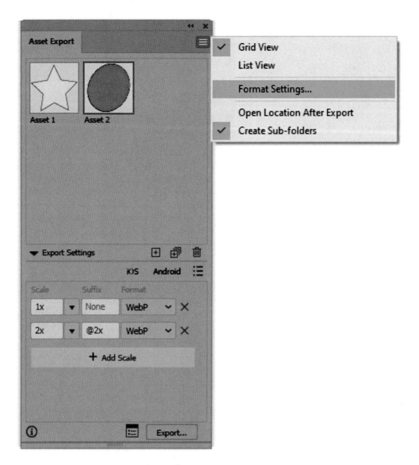

Figure 3-20. *Asset Export panel with menu to access Format Settings*

WebP has some settings that are a combination of PNG, JPEG, and GIF when it comes to quality settings. A WebP file for Image Compression can have minimal or no compression (Lossless) or set a quality of compression (Lossy) 0–100. Other Options for Type Anti-aliasing can include None, Art Optimized (Supersampling), and Type Optimized (Hinted). Refer to Figure 3-21.

Format Settings

PNG
PNG 8
JPG 100
JPG 80
JPG 50
JPG 20
SVG
PDF
WebP

Image Compression

● Lossless
○ Lossy

Quality: ──────────────○ 100   Maximum ∨
        smaller file   larger file

Options

Anti-aliasing: Type Optimized (Hinted) ∨ ⓘ

Background Color: Transparent ∨

☑ Embed ICC Profile: sRGB IEC61966-2.1

(Save Settings) (Cancel)

Figure 3-21. *Format Settings dialog box for WebP Options*

Like PNG and GIF files, you can change the Background Color to Transparent, White, or Black, or Choose Other to access the color picker. Refer to Figure 3-22.

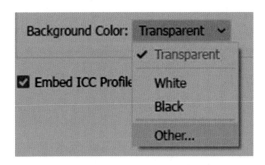

Background Color: Transparent ∨

✓ Transparent

☑ Embed ICC Profile   White

        Black

        Other...

Figure 3-22. *Format Settings dialog box for WebP Options for Background Color*

The embedded ICC Profile is sRGB IEC61966-2.1, so the color mode should be RGB, but web-safe as well. Click the Save Settings button if you plan to alter the default settings, otherwise, click Cancel and exit.

Note that while Illustrator and Photoshop do not have this option, WebP files can be, like GIF files, animated. I will mention how to save a static GIF, if required shortly.

I will just conclude with the panel and mention that once you have altered and reviewed your settings for this and other files, as mentioned here and in Chapter 1, you would then return to the Asset Export panel and click or Shift+click the items you want to export, and click the Export button. Refer to Figure 3-23 and Figure 3-24.

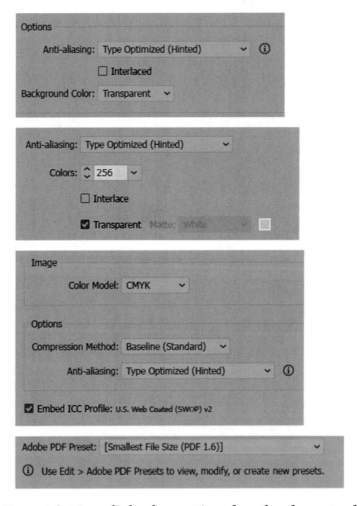

Figure 3-23. *Format Settings dialog box settings for other formats of PNG, PNG8, collectively for JPG (100, 80, 50, 20) and PDF*

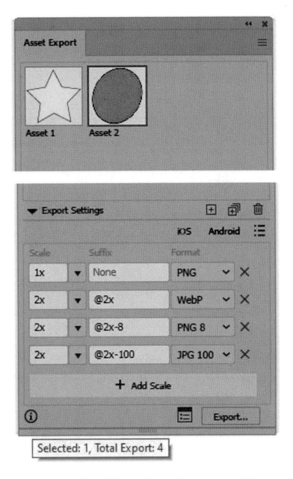

Figure 3-24. *Asset Export panel with various Export setting options set*

You would then pick a location or folder that you want the files to export to on your computer and click the Select Folder button. Refer to Figure 3-25.

Figure 3-25. *Pick Location dialog box with Select Folder button*

Later, if you inspect that folder, you will find that it contains subfolders that have the assets saved and stored within, in the scale setting and formats you assigned. Refer to Figure 3-26.

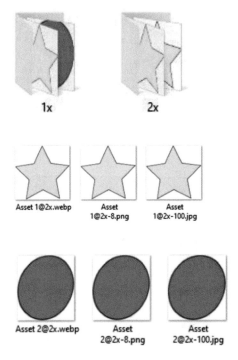

Figure 3-26. Resulting folder and some files created after clicking Export

This is very helpful; however, note that the Asset Export panel does not allow you to save GIF files which you may want to export as well.

Saving GIF Files

If you want to save a static GIF file, you will need to use File ➤ Export ➤ Save for Web (Legacy). Refer to the following figure for more details. Choosing different quality settings from the various preset lists will alter how the colors of the object appear.

Use the Image Size area to scale the image if required. In this case, you would uncheck the setting Clip to Artboard if you only wanted to select the items on the Artboard rather than the whole area. After reviewing the Optimized preview, you would then click save. Refer to Figures 3-27 and 3-28.

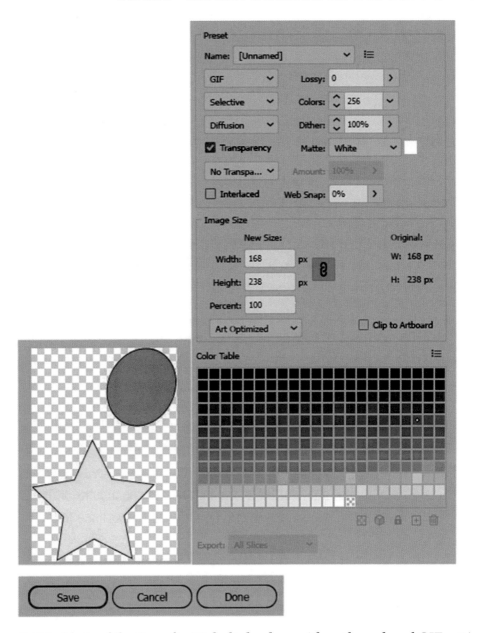

Figure 3-27. *Parts of the Save for Web dialog box with artboard and GIF settings and button options*

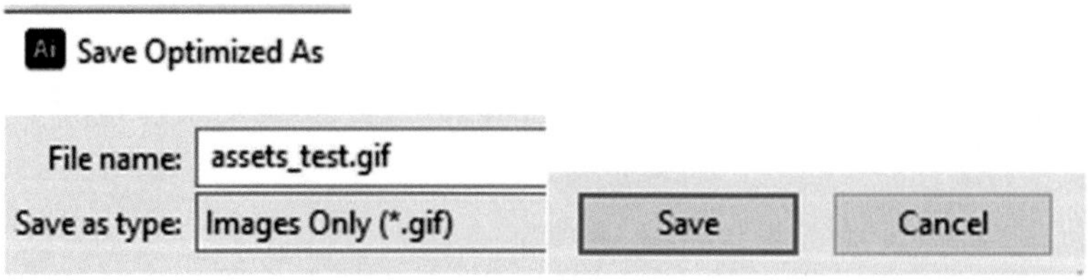

Figure 3-28. *Save Optimized As dialog box Save your gif image on your computer*

In the Save Optimized As dialog box, use the setting Save as type "Images Only (*.gif). Then you would then click Save and save the file in the folder you want to store the GIF file in. Refer to Figure 3-28.

Remember to turn off the layer or sublayer visibility in the Layers panel if you don't want to make certain paths or objects to be part of the GIF file as you do not have the option of selecting individual layers once you are in the dialog box.

Note   You can refer to the following page for more details on Image Optimization using the Save for Web (Legacy) settings on this page, specifically for GIF format, refer to section GIF and PNG-8 Optimization options:

https://helpx.adobe.com/animate/using/optimization-options-for-images-and-animated-gifs.html

While this link is for Animate and not Illustrator, which cannot create animated GIFs, its dialog box shares many of the same settings as the Illustrator and Photoshop Save for Web dialog box and can be used as a reference for specific terms.

Libraries Panel

The last panel that I will discuss in Illustrator is the Libraries panel for sharing and acquiring assets from other Libraries linked to the Creative Cloud Desktop.

The Libraries panel, for the most part, works between your applications Illustrator, Photoshop, InDesign, Animate, Dreamweaver, Bridge, Premiere Pro, and After Effects. Refer to Figure 3-29.

Figure 3-29. *Libraries panel and menu*

They are fairly similar in their layout of the panel, allowing you to import and export various assets that you create in the application, but there are slight differences in what each application's Libraries panel can import or export to another Adobe application.

Note   For InDesign, Animate, and Dreamweaver, rather than being called Libraries panel, the panel is called CC Libraries panel because before the Creative Cloud Libraries panel was introduced, these applications had other Library features or a Libraries panel which has nothing to do with the Creative Cloud connection.

In this case, we are just focusing on Illustrator's Libraries panel, but you can use what you learn here to apply to other Library panels in the other Adobe apps and also refer to the link at the end of this section.

From Illustrator, if you do not have a library started in the panel, you can create one using the panel's menu.

Create a Library

From the Libraries panel's menu, choose Create new library or click the plus icon (+) in the panel. Refer to Figure 3-30.

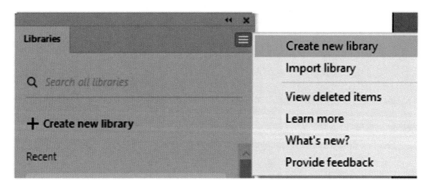

Figure 3-30. *Libraries panel and menu, Create a new library*

Now name your new library and then click the Create button. Refer to Figure 3-31.

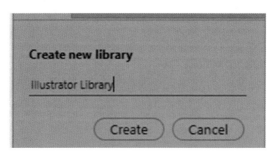

Figure 3-31. *Libraries panel, Create a new library setting*

140

You can now start to add assets from your artboard and other panels to your new library. Refer to Figure 3-32.

Figure 3-32. *Libraries panel, Start building your library*

Add Assets

An Asset can be added either by selecting them and dragging them into the panel as you did with the Asset Export panel or while selecting. You can use the pop-up menu by the plus (+) icon on the lower right to define exactly what part of the asset you want in the library. In this case, it could be when I select a simple star path, just the fill color, stroke color, or the entire graphic. If I click "Add all," this will add the colors (fill and stroke) and the graphic at the same time. Refer to Figure 3-33.

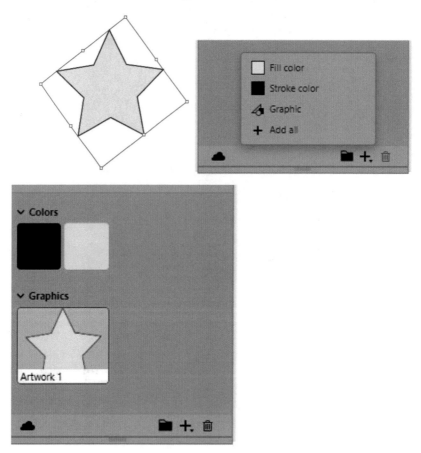

Figure 3-33. *Libraries panel for adding Colors and Graphic assets when an item is selected*

However, with the Libraries panel, you are not limited to just these options (Colors and Graphics), you can also add such things as

- **Colors**: Use the Swatches panel to copy one selected solid swatch at a time to the Libraries panel.

- **Color Themes**: From the Swatches panel color groups (color themes) when they are a collection of 1–5 colors in a folder can be added as a color theme set. For folders with higher color groups of 6 or more, you must select and add the colors separately, one at a time, and these will appear in the colors section. Refer to Figure 3-34 and Figure 3-35.

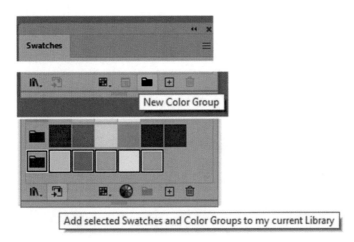

Figure 3-34. *Use the Swatches panel to add color themes*

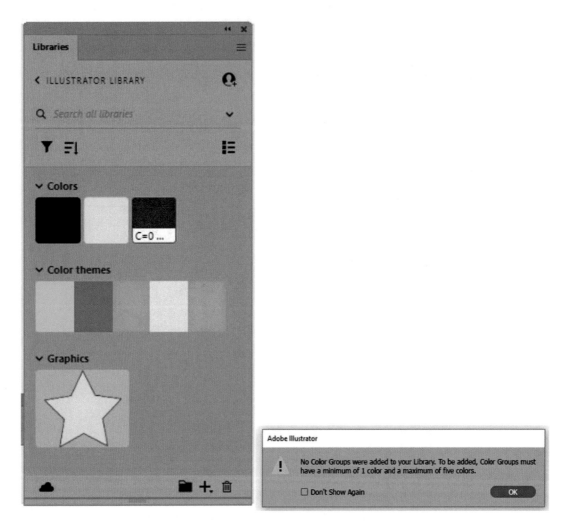

Figure 3-35. *Libraries panel displays color themes and warns you if there are too many colors in the color themes to add from the Swatches panel*

Note   The Adobe Color online app from the Creative Cloud as mentioned in Volume 1 also allows you to acquire and save additional color themes to your libraries outside of Illustrator. These can include your color blind themes. Refer to Volume 1, Chapter 2 for more details. Refer to Figure 3-36.

Figure 3-36. *Adobe Color app link*

Additionally, to a Library, you can add from your artboard:

- **Text Groups**: Which is the block of text when an area of type selected. These can be placed inline if the text is already selected. If no text is selected, then place a copy or place without styles on the Artboard. These options can be accessed when you right-click on the asset in the panel.

- **Character Styles**: Styles applied to individual letters or a word, which can be acquired from a selected area of type. These styles can be applied to selected text or added to the current document when you right-click the asset in the panel.

- **Paragraph Styles**: A style applied to an entire paragraph, which can be acquired from a selected area of type. These styles can be applied or added when you right-click them. These styles can be applied to selected text or added to the current document when you right-click the asset in the panel.

- **Graphics**: Which are grouped and complex with symbol elements that can include gradients, patterns, and other Graphic styles. Refer to Figure 3-37.

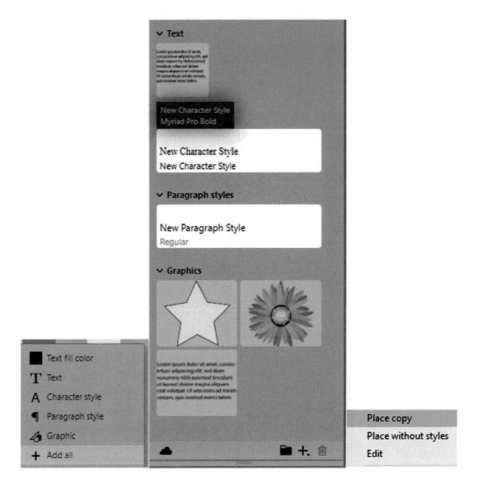

Figure 3-37. *Libraries panel adding Text, Character styles, Paragraph styles, and Graphics assets*

Generally, if Graphics are from the current or another Illustrator collection, you can import (place) them as well by dragging them back onto the Artboard and clicking the location you want to place the graphic. This will place a linked file that is linked to the library. However, if you want to embed the original or see more options, then you need to right-click, for example, the Graphic asset first, and choose Place copy, and click the Artboard to place. Refer to Figure 3-38.

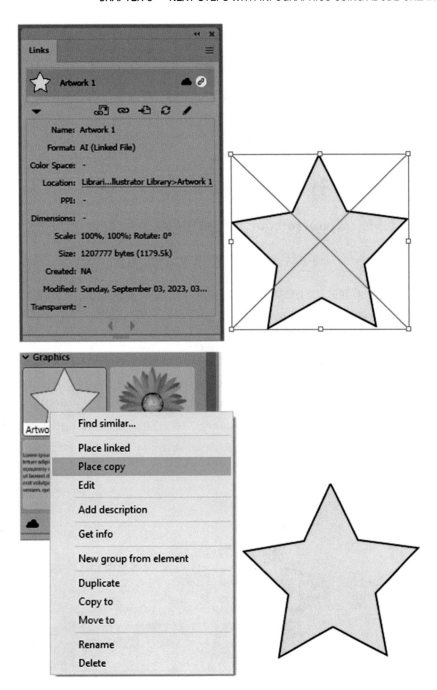

Figure 3-38. *Links panel and Library options for linking or embedding graphics on the Artboard*

By right-clicking a Graphic asset, you can also do things such as Place linked, Edit (to edit in the original application), Duplicate an asset, Copy to and Move to another library, and Rename and Delete (same as trash can icon). Deleting will permanently be removed from the panel unless you click the undo pop-up right away. Refer to Figure 3-39.

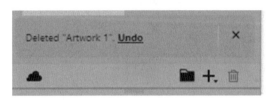

Figure 3-39. *Libraries panel options for undoing the deletion of an asset*

Note   You can also use the menu to Find similar, Add description, and Get info. New group from element is used in the organization of assets.

However, in some instances, you are not limited to assets created solely in Illustrator. You can also import patterns from Photoshop that were created using the Capture in-app extension, exclusively linked to its version of the Libraries panel. They will import as a graphic if dragged onto the Artboard as a placed PNG file or applied automatically to a selected shape when clicked and are automatically applied to the Swatches library. Refer to Figure 3-40.

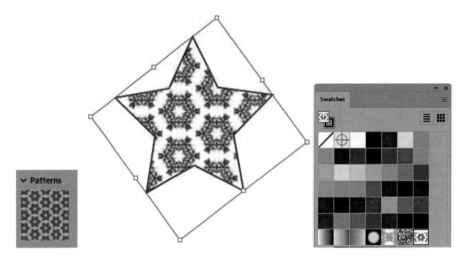

Figure 3-40. *Libraries panel Patterns asset applied to a path and added to the Swatches panel*

And you can acquire Colors and Graphics from Photoshop as well.

Graphics from Photoshop can be linked (Place linked) to the Libraries panel, or you can embed (Place copy) when you right-click them and choose the preferred option and then click on the Artboard. However, note that any graphic from Photoshop will be pixelated and not vector art; if you want to edit it further, use the Control panel to either Image Trace that was discussed in Volume 2 or edit again in Photoshop. Refer to Figure 3-41.

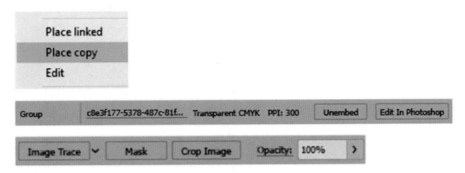

Figure 3-41. *Libraries panel options for an asset from Photoshop and options in the Control panel to edit the placed graphic in Photoshop*

It should be noted that from Photoshop you would not be able to acquire or import a gradient into your Gradient panel or certain Layer styles into your Graphic styles panel, as these are different than Illustrator gradient and Graphic styles, and so remain grayed out and unavailable. This is true of Photoshop brushes as well. Refer to Figure 3-42.

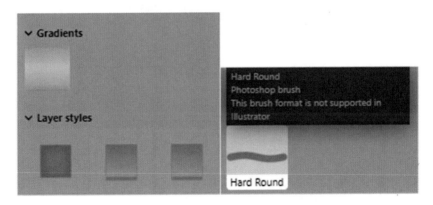

Figure 3-42. *Libraries panel, Gradient, Layer styles, and brushes from Photoshop are not available in Illustrator*

Instead, acquiring these items as part of a graphic will work best.

From Illustrator, Graphic styles cannot be added separately but can be added collectively as part of a graphic which originally could be part of a symbol.

Note that from Animate Libraries, you can acquire brushes that are added to the Brushes panel in Illustrator. Refer to Figure 3-43.

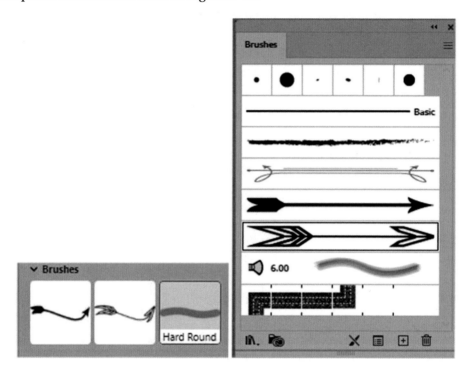

Figure 3-43. *Libraries panel you can acquire brushes from Adobe Animate and add them to the Brushes panel*

Some other important things to note if adding assets from Illustrator to other applications like Photoshop would be

- Graphic assets and character Styles from an Illustrator Library can be imported into Photoshop. Graphics appear in the Layers panel as a smart object layer if linked (cloud icon) or placed (embedded) from the library. Character styles will copy a selection of that type onto a layer when you right-click and choose Use in document. However, it will not allow for Paragraph styles or text unless it is part of the Graphic asset. Refer to Figure 3-44 and Figure 3-45.

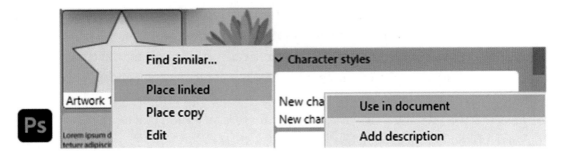

Figure 3-44. *Libraries panel options for placing assets from Illustrator into a Photoshop document*

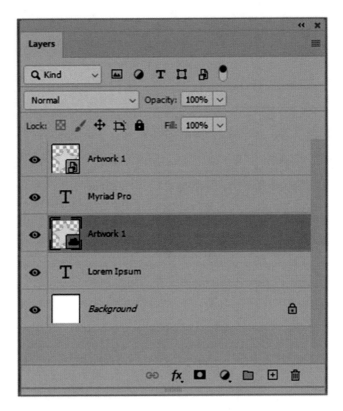

Figure 3-45. *Graphic assets added to the Photoshop Layers panel from Illustrator and the Libraries panel. The cloud icon indicates it is still linked to the Libraries panel*

- InDesign will allow you to add Character and Paragraph styles from an Illustrator Library as well as Colors and Graphic assets.

Other files or assets you would not be able import into Illustrator would be animations from Animate or even Video, Audio, Motion Preset, and Look assets, which might appear present in a library, though other libraries like InDesign would be able to accept the animation. The Libraries guide us when something can or cannot be imported by that asset being grayed out and unavailable. Also, when you right-click the item, this will give you a clue as to whether there is an option that can be linked or copied (embedded). Refer to Figure 3-46.

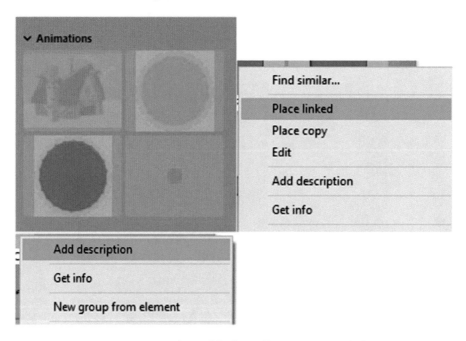

Figure 3-46. *Animation cannot be added to Illustrator and the options of Placed linked and Place copy are removed from the list when you right-click*

Tip   You can use Bridge if you want to add an Illustrator template (ait) to a Library. Refer to Figure 3-47.

Figure 3-47. *Icon for Bridge application*

Bridge I find is sometimes better for adding certain file settings for graphics that you want to import into your library. If you add a file format that Bridge does not support, it will alert you to the file types that it does support, and this can include Adobe Illustrator files like ai and ait, as well as other files for Photoshop or web work like png, bmp, psd, svg, gif, jpg, jpeg, tif, tiff, pdf, and psdt. These you would directly add to a library by dragging them out of Bridge's Content folder into the library. Refer to Figure 3-48 and Figure 3-49.

Figure 3-48. *Use Bridge to add to your current library more advanced files*

However, while not every file format is relevant to this book, there are many other formats being added, which you can add, using Bridge which are for

- **InDesign**: indt

- **Animate Animation**: fla

- **Audio and Video**: heic, heif, dng, mp4, mov, wmv, mpeg, mpg, wav, aac, mp3, mp2, m4a, aiff, aif, and aifc

- **3D and Lighting Files for the Dimension, Substance Collection, and After Effects**: mdl, sbsar, obj, glb, gltf, dn, usdz, ibl, fbx, and exr

- **Library Files**: cclibs and cclibc (Refer to Figure 3-49, then click cancel it exit if you get this warning.)

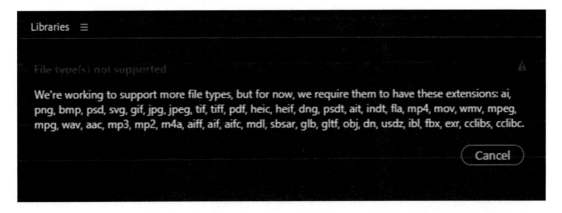

Figure 3-49. *Bridge will warn you when file types cannot be added to a library*

Organize Library Assets

Coming back to Illustrator, as you create various libraries, you will want to keep your assets organized, so make sure to give them descriptive names. You can move out of a current library and search in another by clicking the back left-pointing libraries arrow. Refer to Figure 3-50.

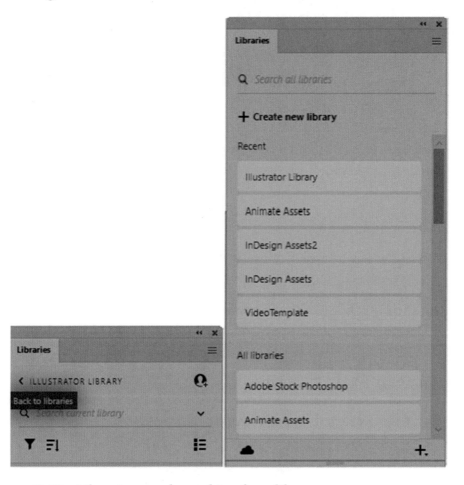

Figure 3-50. *Libraries panel searching for a library*

Here you will be able to see your most recently used libraries and all the libraries, and you can select the one you want to view. Use the search all libraries search area if you need to find a specific file.

Note that the plus (+) icon here will allow you to browse shared libraries which are the ones you may have shared with others. If you have not done this before you will have no current shared libraries However, you can also Go to Stock and Marketplace. Refer to Figure 3-51.

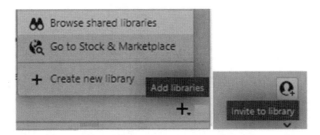

Figure 3-51. *Libraries panel Add libraries and Invite to library options*

If Adobe Stock is part of your paid subscription, it also has many assets such as graphics that you can acquire either for free or an additional price.

Once you select a library, you can also filter the items by colors, graphics, and so on. Refer to Figure 3-52.

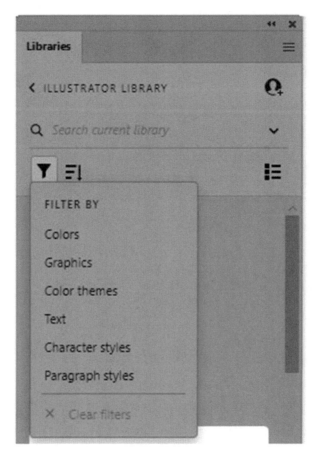

Figure 3-52. *Libraries panel Filter By Options*

Items can be grouped (type or custom group) and sorted (name, custom order, date modified) as well. To create custom groups, use the New group folder at the bottom of the panel. You can create groups and subgroups, and then right-click if you need to ungroup and return to group by Type. Refer to Figure 3-53.

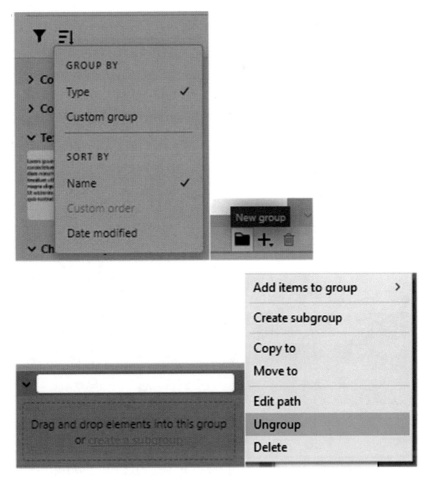

Figure 3-53. *Libraries panel group by options*

Click the view options when you want to view by list or grid. Refer to Figure 3-54.

Figure 3-54. *Libraries panel view options*

Import and Export a Library

To share a library that a client has given you, you can, from the menu, choose Import library and then locate the library you want to import. After you select the library link, locate a file which will be library files (cclibs and cclibc) and click OK. The Import button will become available, and you can add the library to your collection. Refer to Figure 3-55.

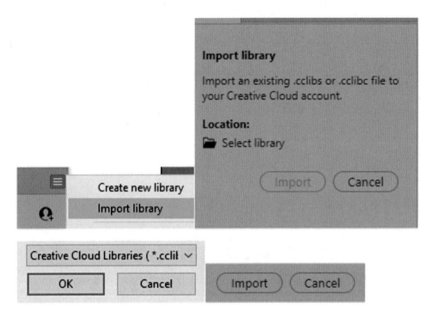

Figure 3-55. *Libraries panel menu import Options and related buttons*

To export a library to share with others, choose Export and the library name. Then select the location on your computer you want to store the file, which could be cclibs and cclibc, depending on your computer. Refer to Figure 3-56.

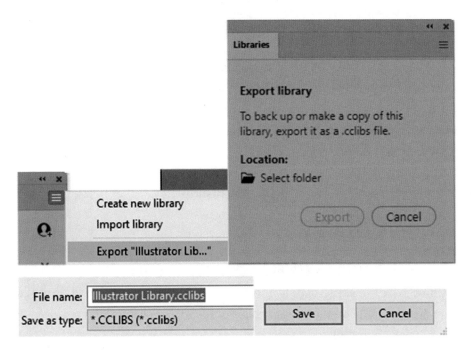

Figure 3-56. *Libraries panel menu Export Options and related buttons*

Click Save and then Export, and Click OK, then you can access this file if you need to email it to a client. Refer to Figure 3-57.

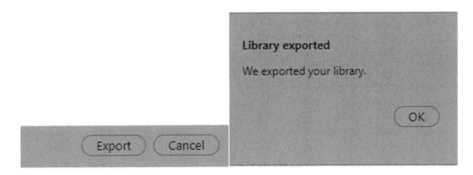

Figure 3-57. *Libraries panel menu Export Options and confirming the Export*

Likewise, this is a good way to keep a backup of your library should you delete it by accident or the cloud is offline and you are unable to recover some files for some reason when it's back online.

Refer to this link for more details on Library creation, inviting people, as well as how to use other Adobe apps with the Libraries panel:

```
https://helpx.adobe.com/creative-cloud/help/libraries.html
```

Layout of Infographics in Photoshop

As we saw in Volume 1 Chapter 3, Photoshop can be used to scan a mock-up that is later recreated in Illustrator. However, in Volume 2, it was mentioned that after designing infographics in Illustrator, we always have the option of taking the design back to Photoshop as Vector Smart Object layers for further enhancement or general editing. Refer to Figure 3-58.

Figure 3-58. *Photoshop application icon*

While we are not going into a lot of detail on this topic, as the focus of this book is on Illustrator, here are some panels, tools, and thoughts to consider to improve an infographic design if you are working with a Photoshop document file or (.psd). Refer to the file cover_page_layout.psd:

- Your Vector Smart Object layer graphic is originally a selected path or grouped path that is Edit ➤ copied from Illustrator and Edit ➤ Pasted into Photoshop. Choose Paste As: Smart Object. Do not choose the option "Add to my current library" unless you want the smart object to add to the Library panel as well and link it to the library; by default; I leave that unchecked. Then I click OK to exit the dialog box. Then click the check in the Options panel to commit the transformation. It can then be incorporated with Photograph or image layers to enhance the layout. Refer to Figure 3-59 and Figure 3-60.

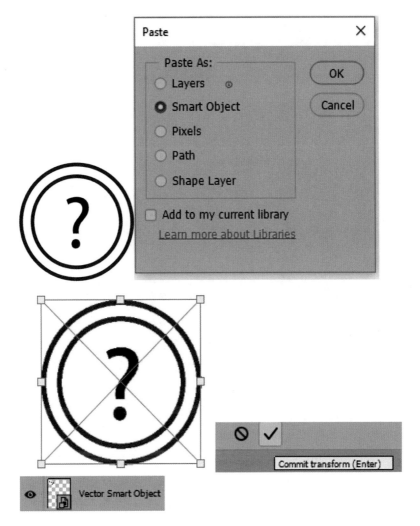

Figure 3-59. *Photoshop options for selecting and copying a grouped path and pasting it into Photoshop as a Vector Smart Object using the Paste dialog box and Options panel*

Figure 3-60. *How the icon appears in Photoshop as part of the start of an infographic cover and in the Layers panel with a photo*

- For your Photoshop projects, always ensure that the resolution is at least 300dpi–600dpi. Make sure to lay out the correct dimensions for the page size of your project when you choose File ➤ New. Refer to Figure 3-61.

8.5 in x 11 in (300 ppi)

Figure 3-61. *Check your document's resolution settings in Photoshop*

- Consider the color mode of your PSD file. Is the final layout in Photoshop to be in RGB or CMYK color mode? Note that in Photoshop with an RGB layout, initially, you will have access to more filter options if you plan to use them. However, to match the RGB Mode, make sure that the Illustrator file with the graphics you are using is converted to RGB Mode first. Else when you copy from an Illustrator file in CMYK mode and paste it into an RGB file in Photoshop as a Vector Smart Object layer, there may be a slight color shift. Refer to the notes in Adobe Illustrator (ai) for more details on converting color modes in Illustrator. Refer to Figure 3-62.

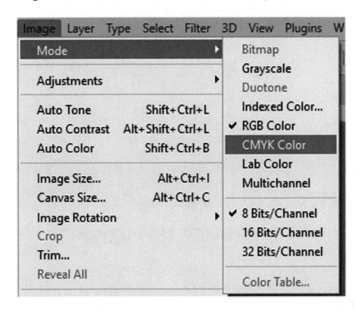

Figure 3-62. *Check your document's color mode settings and use the Image menu to check as well*

Later you can always use Image ➤ Duplicate and click OK to create a copy and then use your Layers panel menu to create a flattened (Layer ➤ Flatten Image) version of your Photoshop file. Refer to Figure 3-63.

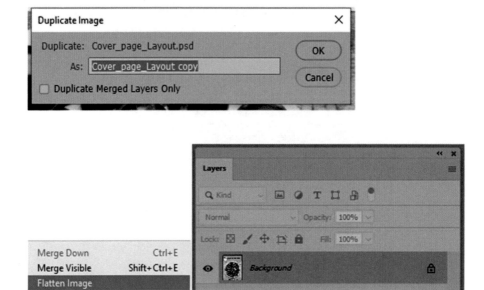

Figure 3-63. *Duplicate Image dialog box, Flatten Image options, and the Layer panel with a background layer*

Then convert it to Image ➤ Mode ➤ CMYK Color Mode if required, and click OK to the warning. Refer to Figure 3-62. Recommended file formats to save your flattened file as could be .tif or .jpeg, but make sure to consult with the print company as to what they prefer as well as on the topic of exact color profile. Refer to Figures 3-62, 3-64, 3-65, and 3-66.

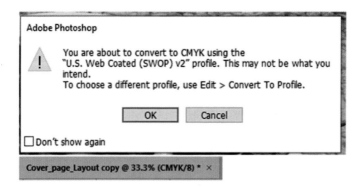

Figure 3-64. *Converting a document to CMYK and the Photoshop warning message*

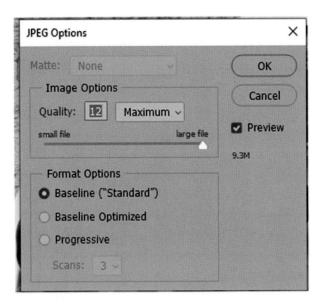

Figure 3-65. *JPEG Options dialog box for saving a copy of the file*

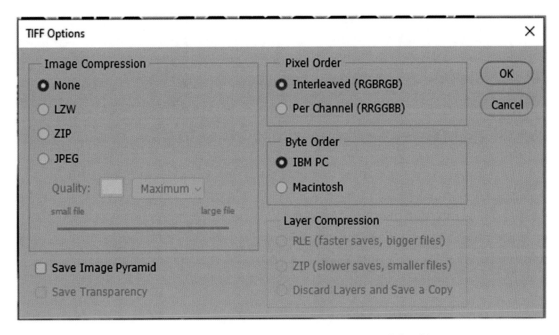

Figure 3-66. *TIFF Options dialog box for saving a copy of the file*

- For your layout while working in your .psd file, apply additional graphic Layer styles using your Layers panel. Some Layer styles may appear more realistic in Photoshop than in Illustrator, and you will find that you will have more layer blending mode options as well. Refer to Figure 3-67.

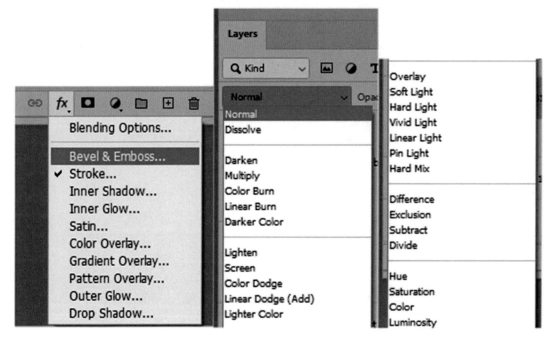

Figure 3-67. *Photoshop Layer styles and blending modes in the Layers panel*

For example, in the mine shaft example from Volume 1, if you were enhancing the design in Photoshop later, as a Vector Smart Object Layer you could add layers painted with the brush tool, and then add a Layer effect of pattern overlay and experiment with different layer blending modes and opacities to give areas of the underground and mined area a more rocklike appearance. You can refer to the file Mining_infographic_texture.psd to explore this idea further. Refer to Figures 3-68, 3-69, and 3-70.

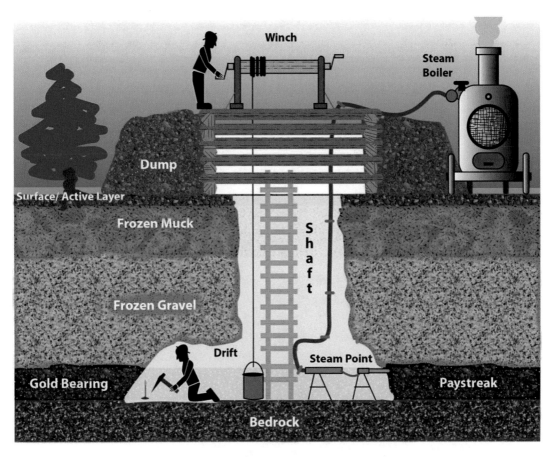

Figure 3-68. *Layer styles applied to the illustration of mine shaft underground*

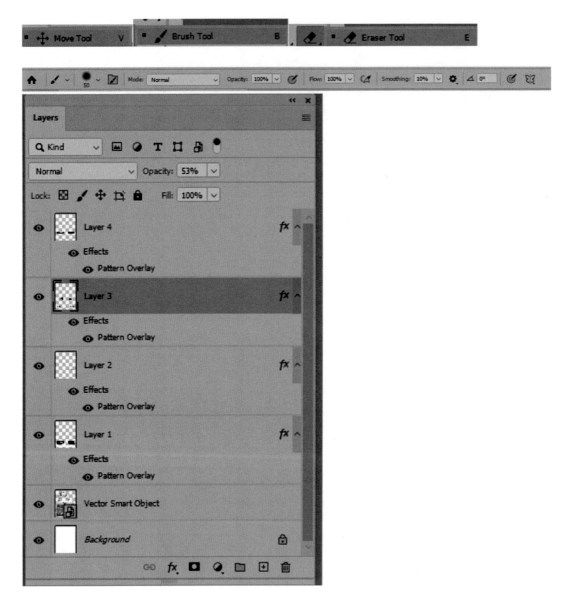

Figure 3-69. *Various Photoshop tools, move tool, brush tool, eraser tool. Control panel and Layers panel*

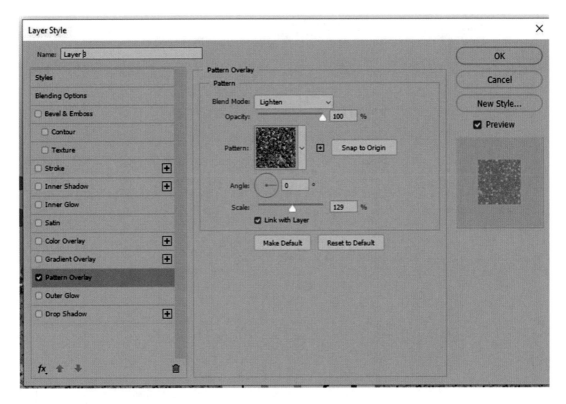

Figure 3-70. *Photoshop Layer Style dialog box with a pattern overlay added and pattern blending mode adjusted*

Tip   In my case for patterns, I used Legacy Patterns and More ➤ Legacy Patterns ➤ Rock Patterns, which you can load from the Patterns panel, if not visible in your Layer Style dialog box. Refer to Figure 3-71.

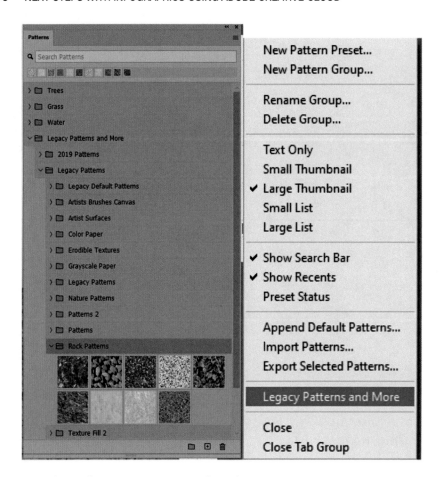

Figure 3-71. *Photoshop Patterns panel and its menu*

- Consider using some of Photoshop's filters to create texture enhancements. The Filter Gallery is a good location, and many of the filters can be added to smart object as smart filters. Refer to Figure 3-72.

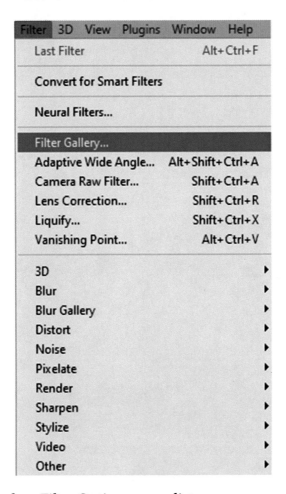

Figure 3-72. *Photoshop Filter Options menu list*

- Whether or not you are using graphic Layer styles or filters in the
  Layers panel, consider using various selection tools to mask and
  hide various areas of your infographic to make the design crisper and
  uniform. For example, a simple layer mask can be accessed from your
  Layers panel if you have a selection active that you created with your
  rectangular Marquee tool by dragging over the image layer. Refer to
  Figure 3-73.

Figure 3-73. *Photoshop Marquee selection tools used with selection enhanced in red, and then a layer mask applied to the selected layer using the Layers panel with the result appearing on the layer itself and the layer effect applied updates*

- Likewise, adjust layers with a selection applied (use the elliptical Marquee tool or Ctrl/CMD+Click on a layer), then apply the adjustment to mask an area. This could be used to change or enhance a selection over part of an infographic (Vector Smart Object layer), and the settings can be adjusted in the Properties panel afterward. Refer to Figures 3-74 and 3-75.

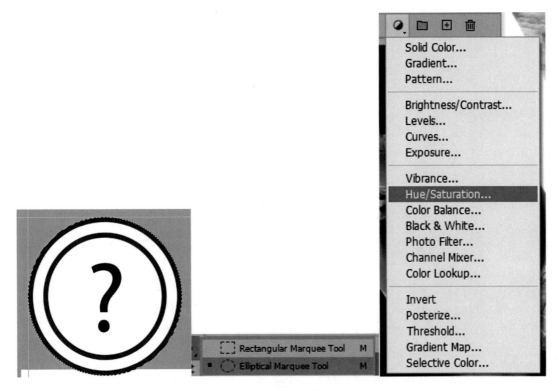

Figure 3-74. *Adding an adjustment layer over the infographic using the Layers panel*

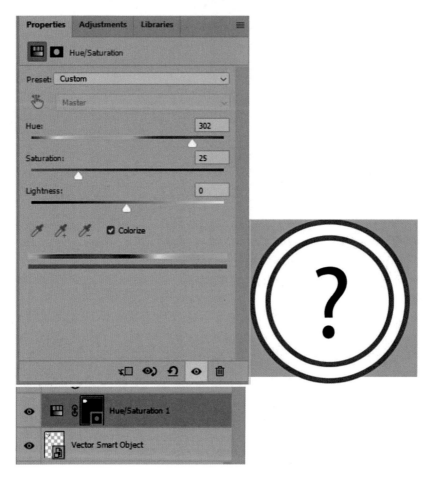

Figure 3-75. *Use the Properties panel to adjust the colors of the adjustment layer and the results in the Layers panel using Hue/Saturation*

- If you want to create a more interactive infographic, consider using the Timeline panel to create a GIF animation or even a video. Refer to Figure 3-76.

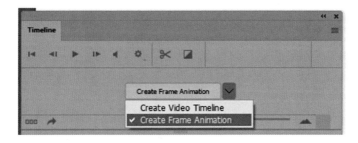

Figure 3-76. *Photoshop Timeline panel*

GIF animations are generally low resolution and have no sound but are good for websites for simple instructions where layers turn on and off to reveal more information at a set duration, much like a slide show. Use the File ➤ Export ➤ Save for Web (Legacy) setting to complete the GIF animation. Refer to the files gif_animation_start.psd and gif_animation_start.gif for reference. Refer to Figures 3-77 and 3-78.

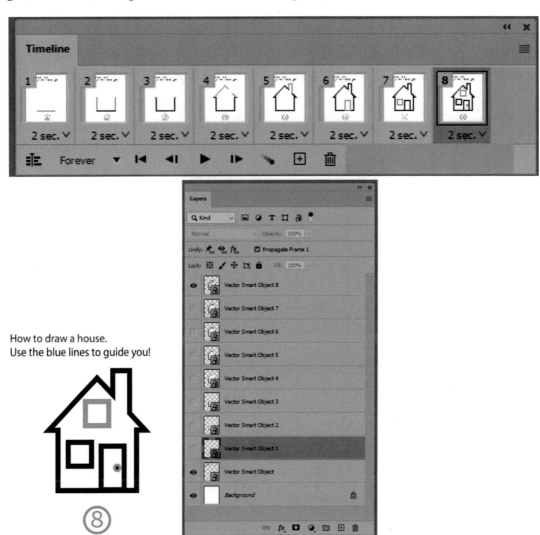

Figure 3-77. *Photoshop Timeline panel and Layers panel with GIF animation added*

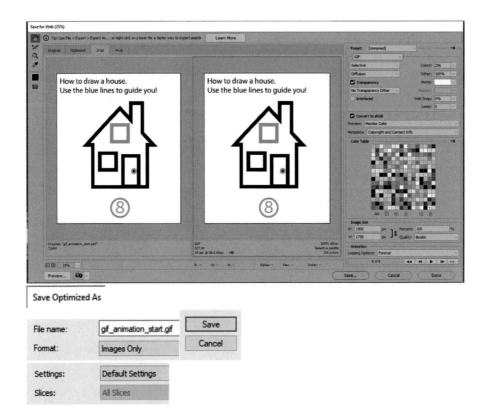

Figure 3-78. *Photoshop's Save for Web dialog box with Animation setting and then Save as Optimized dialog box*

In this case, when you click Save and then Save in the Save Optimized As dialog box, you would make sure the Format is "Images Only," and then Click Save again to complete the transformation.

However, by using the video timeline setting in Photoshop (Figure 3-76), you can produce a higher quality production as well as incorporate sound. These files are usually rendered as .mp4 files, and you may need to use Media Encoder to do some final editing if required. Refer to Figure 3-79.

Figure 3-79. *Media Encoder application icon*

You can learn more about this topic in my books, as mentioned in the introduction, as well as the following page can give you some directions and ideas on this topic:

https://helpx.adobe.com/photoshop/using/new-video-features-photoshop-cs6.html

---

Note   I would not recommend doing any major text layout in Photoshop other than a few keywords or a bold title. I always recommend, if there is a lot of text surrounding the infographic layout, to type text either in Illustrator or link your Photoshop or Illustrator file to an InDesign layout and place the graphic there. Then use InDesign to complete your surrounding text layout.

Layout in InDesign

While not specifically for infographic creation, you can use InDesign files (.indd) for your final layout, whether it is for print or online. Refer to Figure 3-80.

Figure 3-80. *InDesign application icon*

An infographic might be part of a single-page poster layout or spread with surrounding text. Or it might be use with multiple infographics that need step-by-step text instruction. In this next example, you can see how type from an article could be incorporated with the coffee graph from Volume 2, and you can refer to my file coffee_graph_layout.indd. Refer to Figure 3-81.

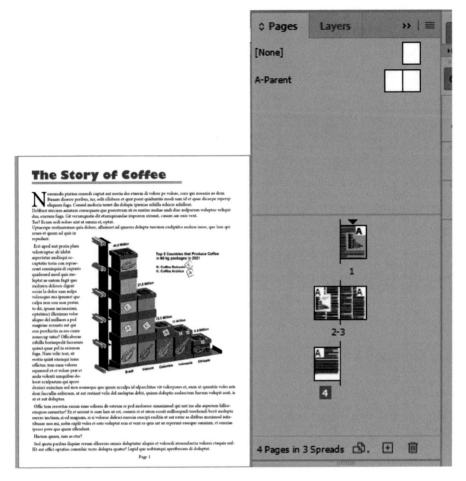

Figure 3-81. InDesign Page Layout example and Pages panel

Print and Type Considerations

Laying out your project in this application is ideal when you have large amounts of text, such as when the infographic or multiple infographics will part of a newsletter, magazine, or booklet. This is always the best solution as you can see all your pages at a glance using your Pages panel.

In this case, using File ➤ Place the Placed/linked Image of the graph that I used, was before being added to InDesign, copied and pasted into Photoshop as Vector Smart Object layer, and then the layer was flattened. Then I saved a final file as a .tif file format so that this design would render correctly. This is important to consider if you find that the 3D file that you created in Illustrator is not displaying as it should. While 2D files from Illustrator will generally render and display correctly, often files that are drawn in Illustrator that have a lot of gradients or 3D effects may not. So, in these situations, it is always good to flatten the final graphic using Photoshop and save the file as a .tiff. This is ideal in situations where it is not critical to have a transparent background surrounding the graphic. Refer to the section in this chapter "Layout of Infographics in Photoshop" if you need to review this as you can repeat this same process for any Vector Smart Object from Illustrator. You can see that the file is linked using the Links panel. Refer to Figure 3-82.

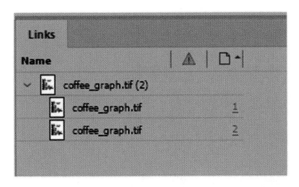

Figure 3-82. *InDesign Links panel*

Type, in this case, is often typed using the Type Tool, into a Text frame, that you drag out with the Type Tool to create an area as you do in Illustrator. Refer to Figure 3-83.

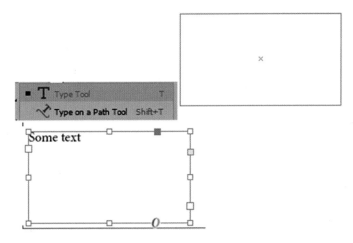

Figure 3-83. *InDesign Type Tool and Text frame area with some text typed*

These text frames can be linked as well to each other for more text to flow onto another page.

Similarities Between Illustrator and InDesign

Once you have learned how to use Illustrator successfully, learning the application InDesign is quite easy to start working with as there are many of the same tools and similar panels in each program. Examples would be the Selection Tool, Direct Selection Tool, pen tools, and type tools found in InDesign's tools panel, as well as the Control, Properties, and CC Libraries panel mentioned earlier in this chapter. Refer to Figure 3-84.

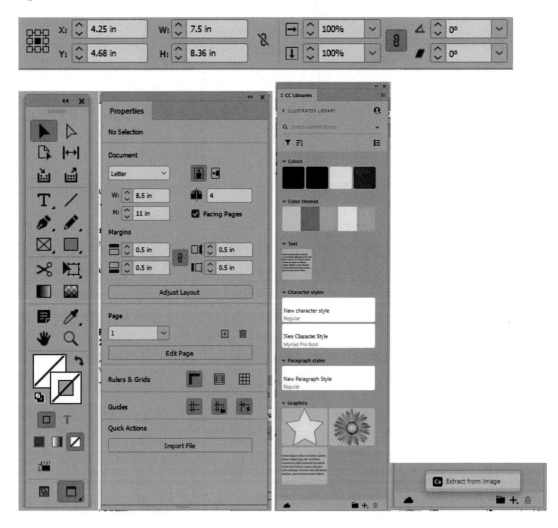

Figure 3-84. *InDesign panels, Control, Tools, Properties, and CC Libraries with Extract from Image Option*

Note   In reference to the Libraries panel, InDesign does have a feature that is part of the Capture in-app extension that does allow you to "Extract from Image" color themes, shapes, and type. Refer to Figure 3-84.

However, one helpful panel that I often rely on is the Text Wrap panel, which allows the frame around your infographic to push the text in the text boxes away from the image so that text does not run behind the infographic by mistake. The option used here is called "Wrap around bounding box." Refer to Figures 3-85 and 3-86.

Uptaerspe restiuntotam quia dolore, ullamust ad quaeres dolupta tureium endipides andam imus, que lam qui renes et quam ad quis in repudant.

Erit aped unt pratia plam velestruptae ab idebit asperiatur andisqui occuptatio toria con repraeceari omnisquia di cuptatis quidessed mod quis moluptat as entem fugit quo moloren delesen digent occae la dolor sam nulpa volesequo ma ipsumet que culpa non con non pratur, to dit, ipsam incimaximi, optatiusci illenimus volor aliquo del millaces a ped magniae rernatis aut qui con perchictis as eos cume nonecup tatur? Officaborae nihilla boriaspedit facearum quisci quae pel in erionem fuga. Nam velic tent, sit eostia quiat eiumqui iume offictur, tem eum volores equassed et et volore prat et anda volenti umquibus dolorat eculparum qui apero

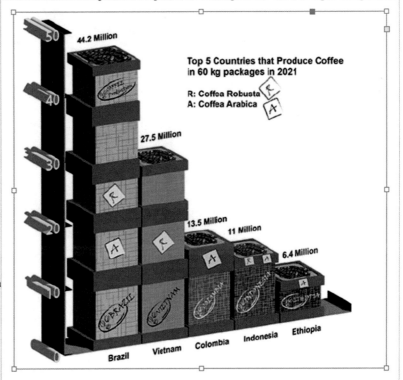

denisci eniscium sed mos nonseque que quam acculpa id ulparchitae vit volorpores et, eum ut quuntiis voles aris dem faccullis eriberum, ut aut restiant velis del moluptas debit, quiam doluptis andaectem harum volupit assit, is ut et aut doluptus.

Figure 3-85.   *InDesign with Image Frame and Text Wrap applied*

Figure 3-86. *InDesign's Text Wrap Panel*

For more information on working in InDesign, you can visit this page:
`https://helpx.adobe.com/support/indesign.html`

Print as a PDF

Afterward the document could be exported as a PDF using File ➤ Export ➤ and saved as
Adobe PDF (Print) and then emailed to a client. This file could later be printed or placed
on a website. Refer to Figure 3-87.

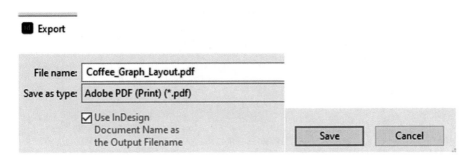

Figure 3-87. *Export Options dialog box settings Save as type Adobe PDF(Print) (.pdf)*

Note   The other option, which is not discussed in this book, is Adobe PDF (Interactive) which is for creating interactive forms.

After clicking Save, you will be presented with a very similar dialog box with tabs as you saw for creating PDFs using Illustrator. However, now you are working with a more complex document which will have some additional settings in the General, Compression, Marks and Bleeds, Output, Advanced, Security, and Summary tabs as they relate to InDesign. Refer to Figure 3-88.

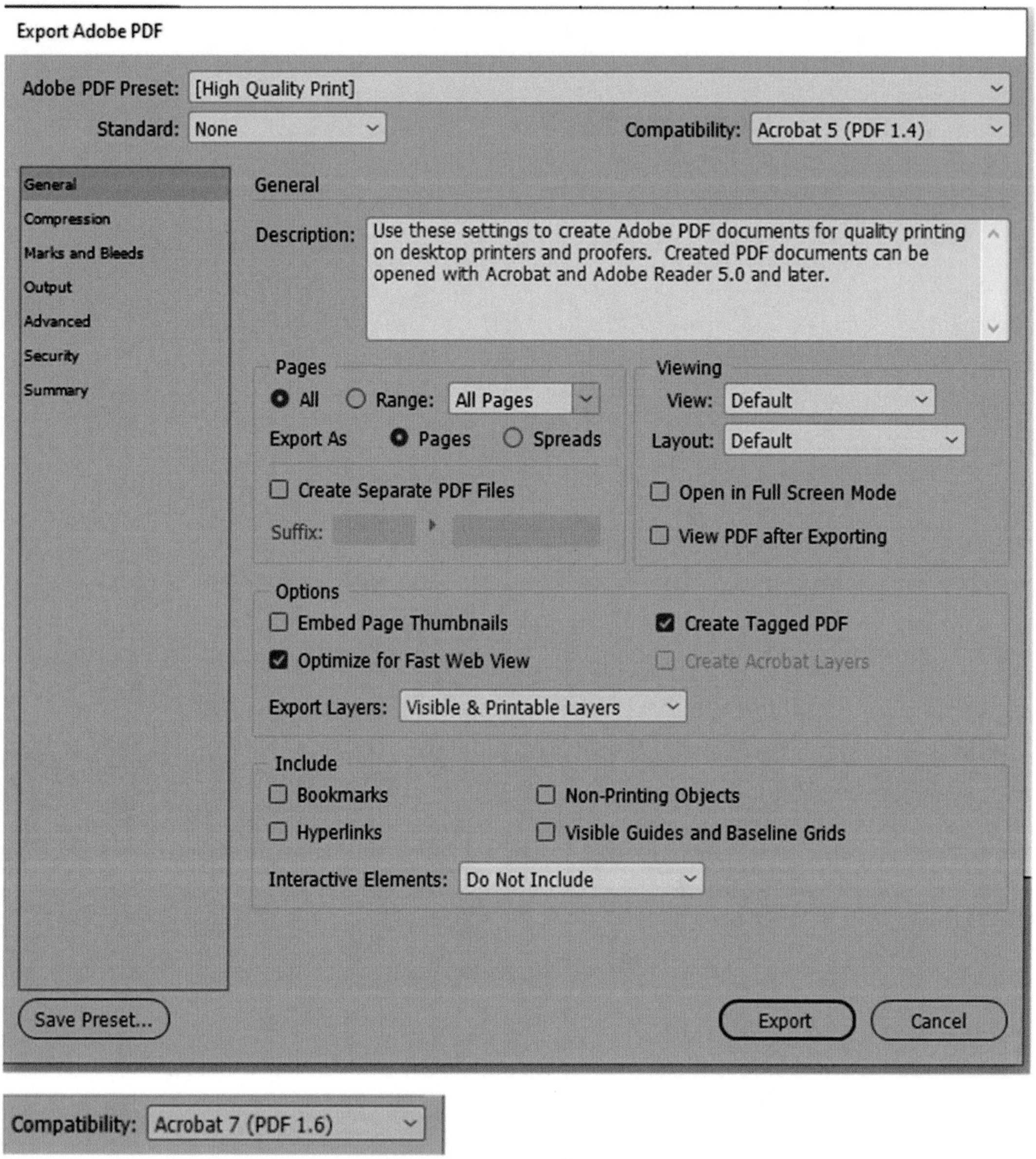

Figure 3-88. *Export Adobe PDF dialog box in the General tab*

For now, leave at the default settings, and click Export to create the PDF in a location on your computer. However, you should consult with your printing company if you are unsure of specific settings before sending the final PDF. One area you may want to increase is your compatibility setting in the upper right as note in Illustrator where it was set at Acrobat 7 (PDF 1.6).

For more information on Export PDF settings from InDesign, refer to this page: `https://helpx.adobe.com/indesign/using/exporting-publishing-pdf.html`

Layout in Animate

Animate is a good program to learn if you want to create simple animations for a website, and after learning Photoshop and Illustrator, you can apply many of the skills learned in those applications to the tools and panels in this application.

Like Photoshop, Animate can be used to create GIF animations, but also more complex ones using the HTML5 canvas (OAM packages) and MP4 video files. Refer to Figure 3-89.

Figure 3-89. *Animate and Media Encoder dialog boxes for applications*

Note   GIF animations cannot have sound while OAM and MP4 files can.

For creating an animate GIF, you would use File ➤ Export ➤ Export Animated GIF.

For video: File ➤ Export ➤ Video/Media

HTML5 canvas and OAM files are published under the File ➤ Publish Settings area.

When creating a video file for the Web, as mentioned, you may need to use Media Encoder to create the final (MP4) document from Animate (.fla) file as it has to first become a (.mov) movie before converting to a (.mp4).

Rather than just use SVG files from Illustrator, you can add further interactivity using the Timeline panel and various keyframes that are tied to Symbols on the Artboard and in the Library panel. These keyframes could be expanded using the timeline if more time is required or if it runs too quickly. Refer to Figure 3-90 and Figure 3-91.

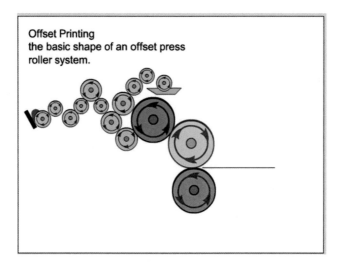

Figure 3-90. *Animated Graphic in Animate to represent the Offset Printing rollers*

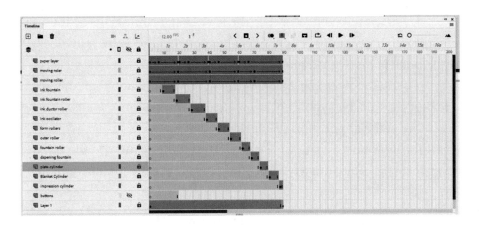

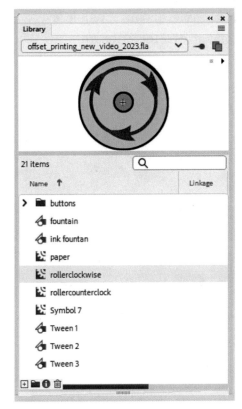

Figure 3-91. *Animate Timeline panel and Library panel*

In this case, you would need to refer to the file offset_printing_new_video_2023.fla as it is impossible, on the static page, to fully visualize the interactivity involved. It would take an entire book to discuss Animate basics as well as the different kinds of fla files used, which are HTML canvas and ActionScript3.0. I will mention that ActionScript3.0 files are the best choice when you want to create GIF animations or video files because you can use more of the application's features.

To review the final video example, refer to offset_printing_new_video_2023.mp4.

However, I will just point out a few key things as they relate to Illustrator and Photoshop:

- Animate, I find, is much better than Photoshop for controlling your GIF animation using its Timeline panel as it contains multiple layers and keyframes that you can easily organize on the Artboard.

- Animate has many similarities to Illustrator, and simple vector shapes can be easily copied and pasted from Illustrator directly into Animate with many of the settings intact. Refer to Figure 3-92.

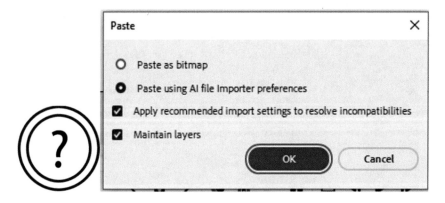

Figure 3-92. *Animate options for Paste dialog box*

If the object in Illustrator was already assigned as a Symbol and is in the Symbols panel, then, when copied and pasted, it will automatically, upon clicking OK in Animate, be added to the Library panel. Refer to Figure 3-93.

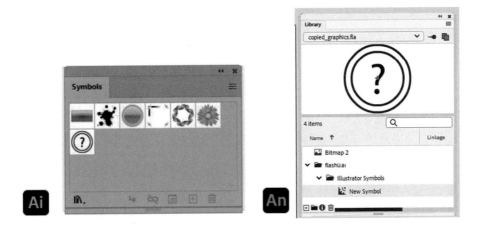

Figure 3-93. *Adobe Illustrator Symbols panel and when pasted in Animate appears in Library panel*

- Animate does have similar selection tools, drawing tools, like shapes, pen tools, and type tools as well as a Properties panel. However, I find it much easier to create all the shapes for my animation in Illustrator first and then copy and paste them directly into Animate. Refer to Figure 3-94.

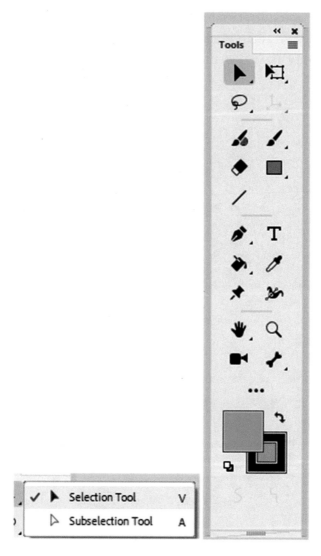

Figure 3-94. *Animate Tools, Selection Tool and Subselection Tool*

- As well, you can copy and paste directly a selection on a rasterized
  layer from Photoshop and add these as Library items to Animate. In
  the case of Photoshop, the images will paste directly in as a bitmap
  file. Refer to Figure 3-95.

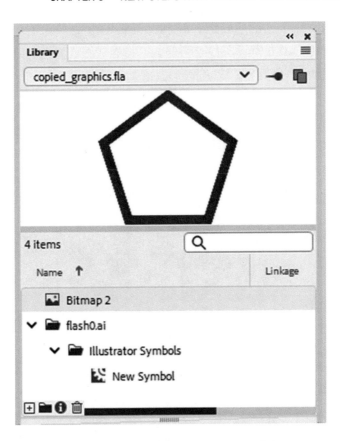

Figure 3-95. *Animate Library panel with Bitmap graphic*

- Another way to add images from Photoshop or Illustrator files is to use File ➤ Import ➤ Import to Stage or File ➤ Import ➤ Import to Library.

- Keep in mind that regardless if the image comes from Photoshop or Illustrator, if you add various graphic and filter effects to the image, because the animation is meant for low-resolution web design (72ppi), some more detailed graphics will appear blurry and may not reproduce as you intend. For Illustrator, when pasting, choosing the option to paste as bitmap may be the best solution, or you may have to simplify the artwork.

- As mentioned earlier, you can also acquire colors, color themes, and graphics from the CC Libraries panel. Also, you can export animations. Refer to Figure 3-96.

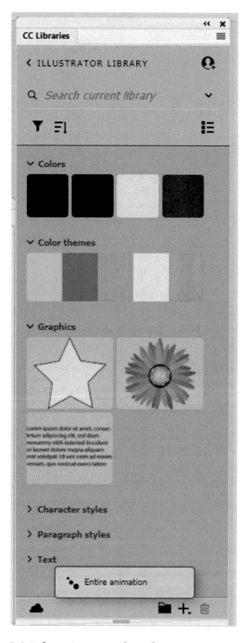

Figure 3-96. *Animate CC Libraries panel with options to import an entire animation*

Later in Animate, you can continue to edit and modify your shapes and symbols for various effects, such as motions and color visibilities, blends, and filters on the Timeline.

- If you are going for a more high-quality resolution that involves photos and live action, consider creating your animation and video layout in applications like Premiere Pro and After Effects, which I will mention in a moment.

- For more details on Animate, you can refer to the following page:

  https://helpx.adobe.com/support/animate.html

Dreamweaver for the Web

As we saw earlier in Chapter 1, you can use Illustrator to create your (SVG) file and then later add it to an HTML page as part of the interactivity. Refer to Figure 3-97.

Figure 3-97. *Dreamweaver icon for application*

However, if you are doing a lot of charts and graphs, then you will want to learn more about HTML5 canvas, jQuery, or other related JavaScript coding like "Ploty.js," "Chart.js," "Graph Google," and "D3.js" that can make your charts and graphics more interactive online and edit in real time which is good for updating if the data changes quickly.

Some links on that topic you may want to explore and research for your next project:

https://canvasjs.com/jquery-charts/
www.w3schools.com/ai/ai_graphics.asp
www.w3schools.com/ai/ai_canvas.asp
www.w3schools.com/ai/ai_chartjs.asp
www.w3schools.com/ai/ai_plotly.asp
www.w3schools.com/ai/ai_google_chart.asp
www.w3schools.com/ai/ai_d3js.asp

Code like this can be copied and added to an HTML5 page using Dreamweaver and edited in the application further.

Note   You can use Dreamweaver to add videos such as .MP4 which can also be linked to your HTML pages using the HTML5 video option in code view and with its Properties panel. While not a topic in this book, you can find out more on this topic in my book mentioned in the introduction as well as the following link:

```
https://helpx.adobe.com/dreamweaver/using/insert-html5-
video.html
```

As mentioned earlier, in the chapter, you can also acquire graphics, colors, and color themes for Dreamweaver using its CC Libraries panel. However, unlike other panels, you cannot add to the library any assets. Refer to Figure 3-98.

Figure 3-98. *Dreamweaver CC Libraries panel*

Video (Premiere Pro and After Effects)

Keep in mind that for video, Adobe has Premiere Pro and After Effects that you can use to further enhance your interactive story and incorporate the infographic. Note that Audition is usually added to this section for audio as well. Refer to Figure 3-99.

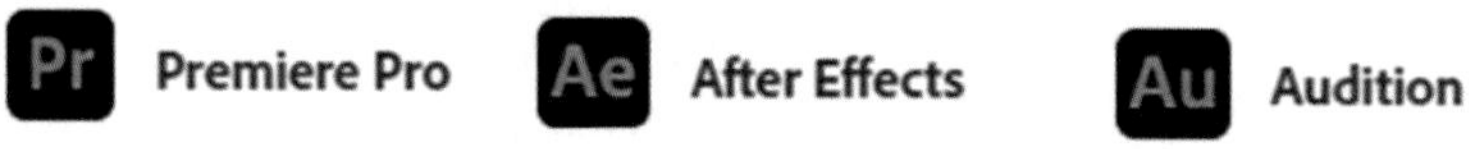

Pr Premiere Pro   **Ae** After Effects   **Au** Audition

Figure 3-99. *Premiere Pro, After Effects, and Audition icons for applications*

Here are some links to more information on those applications:

```
https://helpx.adobe.com/support/premiere-pro.html
https://helpx.adobe.com/support/after-effects.html
https://helpx.adobe.com/support/audition.html
```

Adobe 3D Applications

Also, besides using Illustrator in Volume 2 for 3D design, Adobe also has the Substance collection for enhancing and creating 3D assets. These include Areo (Beta), Substance 3D Painter, Sampler, Designer, Stager, and Modeler. These products can be added to your current plan if you do not have them as part of your Creative Cloud desktop applications. Refer to Figure 3-100.

Ar Aero (Beta)   **Pt** Substance 3D Painter   **Sa** Substance 3D Sampler

Ds Substance 3D Designer   **Sg** Substance 3D Stager

Md Substance 3D Modeler

Figure 3-100. *Substance Collection Options Aero, Painter, Sampler, Designer, Stager and Modeler*

You can learn more about these from the following pages:

```
www.adobe.com/creativecloud/3d-ar/campaign/pricing.html
www.adobe.com/products/aero.html
```

Adobe XD and Adobe Express

You can now use these other desktop and mobile applications for creating charts as they relate to prototyping applications. Refer to Figure 3-101.

 XD   Adobe Express

Figure 3-101. *XD and Adobe Express application icons*

Here are some links on that topic:

www.adobe.com/products/xd/learn/prototype/auto-animate/create-animated-charts.html

www.adobe.com/express/create/chart

Summary

In this chapter, we looked at some of the options that you have for exporting and saving files in various formats from Illustrator and reviewed the Asset Export and Libraries panels.

Then we reviewed, briefly, additional Adobe applications that are part of the Creative Cloud that you can use to take your infographic to the next level.

I hope that these volumes and chapters and the various projects have given you a better understanding of the process of designing infographics and this will inspire you as you create your next project.

Index

A

© Jennifer Harder 2023
J. Harder, *Creating Infographics with Adobe Illustrator: Volume 3*,
https://doi.org/10.1007/979-8-8688-0038-2

T, U

V, W, X, Y, Z

Printed in the United States
by Baker & Taylor Publisher Services